BROADMAN COMMENTS JAN.-MAR.'97

13 Ready-To-Teach Bible Study Lessons

13 Ready-To-Teach Bible Study Lessons

ROBERT J. DEAN
J. B. FOWLER, JR.
JAMES E. TAULMAN

Based on the International Sunday School Lessons
Each Plan Includes These Sections: ❁ Studying the Bible
❁ Applying the Bible ❁ Teaching the Bible

BROADMAN
& HOLMAN
PUBLISHERS

Nashville, Tennessee

This material was first published in *Broadman Comments, 1996–1997*

4217-45
ISBN: 0-8054-1745-1

Dewey Decimal Classification: 268.61
Printed in the United States of America

Broadman Comments *is published quarterly by Broadman & Holman Publishers, 127 Ninth Avenue, North, Nashville, Tennessee 37234*

When ordered with other church literature, it sells for $4.99 per quarter. Second class postage paid at Nashville, Tennessee

ISSN: 0068-2721

POSTMASTER: Send address change to *Broadman Comments,* Customer Service Center, 127 Ninth Avenue, North Nashville, Tennessee 37234

WRITERS

STUDYING THE BIBLE

Robert J. Dean continues the theological traditions of *Broadman Comments* while adding his own fresh insights. Dean is retired from the Baptist Sunday School Board, and is a Th.D. graduate of New Orleans Seminary

APPLYING THE LESSON

J. B. Fowler, Jr. is a freelance writer from San Antonio, Texas. He was formerly editor of *Baptist New Mexican* of the New Mexico Baptist Convention.

TEACHING THE CLASS

James E. Taulman is a freelance writer in Nashville, Tennessee. Prior to that, Taulman was an editor of adult Sunday school materials for the Baptist Sunday School Board.

ABBREVIATIONS AND TRANSLATIONS

Scripture passages are from the authorized King James Version of the Bible. Other translations used:

NASB   From the New American Standard Bible. © The Lockman Foundation, 1960, 1962, 1963, 1968, 1971, 1972, 1973, 1975, 1977. Used by Permission.

NIV   From the Holy Bible, New International Version. Copyright © 1973, 1978, 1984 by International Bible Society. Used by permission.

RSV   From The Revised English Bible. Copyright © Oxford University Press and Cambridge University Press, 1989. Reprinted by permission.

NRSV   From the New Revised Standard Version of the Bible, copyright © 1989 by the Division of Christian Education of the National Council of Churches of Christ in the United States of America. Used by permission. All rights reserved.

Contents

NEW TESTAMENT PERSONALITIES

January

PERSONS IN JESUS' MINISTRY

Jan. 5 — John the Baptizer 2

Jan. 12 — Mary and Martha 9

Jan 19 — Peter 17

Jan 26 — Judas Iscariot 25

February

PERSONS OF THE NEW TESTAMENT CHURCH

Feb. 2 — Barnabas..................................... 32

Feb. 9 — Stephen...................................... 40

Feb. 16 — Priscilla and Aquila 47

Feb. 23 — Timothy 55

HOPE FOR THE FUTURE (1 and 2 Thessalonians)

March

STAND FAST IN THE LORD

Mar. 2 — Proclaim the Gospel! 62

Mar. 9 — Live in Love and Holiness..................... 69

Mar. 16 — Pray for Others! 76

Mar. 23 — Do What Is Right! 83

Mar. 30 — The Resurrection Hope 90

Alternative lesson for January 19th

Jan. 19 — Respect for Human Life...................... 97

New Testament Personalities

(January/February)

INTRODUCTION

January and February studies focus on key personalities in the New Testament. January's studies portray "Persons in Jesus' Ministry." These lessons focus on John the Baptist as the forerunner of Jesus; Mary and Martha as loyal friends of Jesus; Peter; who confessed Jesus as the Messiah and then rebuked Jesus for talking about His death; and Judas, who betrayed Jesus.

February's studies are entitled "Persons of the New Testament Church." The first lesson cites several examples of Barnabas as an encourager. The second lesson presents Stephen, the first Christian martyr. Lesson three is about Paul's loyal friends Priscilla and Aquila. Lesson four is about Timothy, whom Paul considered his son in the faith.

• Note: There is an alternative lesson provided for January 19 on page 97 for those desiring to teach the "Sanctity of Human Life" study.

Hope for the Future (1 and 2 Thessalonians,)

(March)

INTRODUCTION

March's lessons cover selected passages in 1 and 2 Thessalonians. Paul reminded his readers of how he had proclaimed the gospel to them. He challenged them to lives of love and holiness. He commended their faithfulness and prayed for them. He challenged them to earn their own living. The Easter lesson combines Matthew 28:1–10 on the resurrection of Christ with 1 Thessalonians 4:13–18 on the resurrection of believers.

John the Baptizer

Basic Passages: Mark 1:1–15; Luke 7:18–30
Focal Passages: Mark 1:4–11, 14–15; Luke 7:18–23

This lesson begins a four-lesson study on "Persons in Jesus' Ministry." John the Baptist (literally "Baptizer") was born to be the forerunner of Jesus (see the lesson for Dec. 1). John's bold preaching of repentance and his baptism drew crowds, which he pointed to One mightier than he. After John was arrested, Jesus began His own ministry—a ministry that at times puzzled John.

▶**Study Aim:** *To describe how John the Baptist set the stage for the ministry of Jesus*

STUDYING THE BIBLE

OUTLINE AND SUMMARY
   I. The Beginning of the Gospel (Mark 1:1–15)
      1. The gospel and John's ministry (1:1–6)
      2. John and the One mightier than he (1:7–8)
      3. Baptism of Jesus (1:9–11)
      4. Temptations of Jesus (1:12–13)
      5. Jesus preaching the gospel (1:14–15)
  II. When John Was in Prison (Luke 7:18–30)
      1. John's question (7:18–20)
      2. Jesus' answer (7:21–23)
      3. Jesus' commendation of John (7:24–30)

John the Baptist prepared for the Messiah by preaching repentance and baptizing those who repented (Mark 1:1–6). John pointed to One mightier than he, who would baptize with the Holy Spirit (Mark 1:7–8). When Jesus was baptized, the Spirit descended on Him and a voice from heaven declared Him to be God's Son and Servant (Mark 1:9–11). Jesus was driven into the wilderness by the Spirit, where he was tempted by Satan, after which angels ministered to Him (Mark 1:12–13). After John's arrest, Jesus preached that people should repent and believe because the kingdom was at hand (Mark 1:14–15). From prison John sent his disciples to ask Jesus if He was the coming One, or should they look for another (Luke 7:18–20). Jesus told John's disciples to describe Jesus' ministry of healing, helping, and preaching to John (Luke 7:21–23). Jesus commended John as more than a prophet, but noted that he did not see the fulfillment of the kingdom to which he had pointed (Luke 7:24–30).

I. Beginning of the Gospel (Mark 1:1–15)

1. The gospel and John's ministry (1:1–6)

The Gospel of Mark is introduced with the words, "The beginning of the gospel of Jesus Christ, the Son of God" (v. 1). Mark's account of the gospel begins with the work of John the Baptist, who fulfilled Malachi 3:1 and Isaiah 40:3 (vv. 2–3).

4 John did baptize in the wilderness, and preach the baptism of repentance for the remission of sins.

5 And there went out unto him all the land of Judaea [joo DEE uh], and they of Jerusalem, and were all baptized of him in the river of Jordan, confessing their sins.

John's ministry focused on preaching repentance and baptizing those who repented. Luke 3:7–14 gives an example of his preaching. He called on people to turn from their sins, and he expected them to begin to do what was right. John's mission was to prepare the way for the Messiah. He called on people to prepare themselves by repenting of their sins and receiving God's forgiveness. As a sign of their repentance and forgiveness, John baptized them in the Jordan River.

Judaism had a number of washings, but the closest thing to John's baptism was proselyte baptism. When Gentiles were converted to Judaism, they were required to be baptized. This baptism was only for Gentile converts, and John insisted that Jews also needed to repent and be baptized. Gentile converts immersed themselves, whereas John immersed those who came to him in repentance. This seems to be where he got his name "the baptizer."

6 And John was clothed with camel's hair, and with a girdle of a skin about his loins; and he did eat locusts and wild honey;

Luke 1:80 tells us that John lived in the wilderness from an early age. His food was what he could forage in that bleak region. His clothing and appearance reminded people of Elijah the prophet (2 Kings 1:8). Malachi 4:5–6 had predicted that God would send Elijah the prophet before the day of the Lord. John was the fulfillment of that promise.

2. John and the One mightier than he (1:7–8)

7 And preached, saying, there cometh one mightier than I after me, the latchet of whose shoes I am not worthy to stoop down and unloose.

8 I indeed have baptized you with water: but he shall baptize you with the Holy Ghost.

When John preached, he pointed beyond himself to One mightier than he. A slave or servant would unloose the latchet of a guest's sandals, but John said that he was unworthy to serve the coming One even in such a lowly way. John said that his baptism in water foreshadowed a baptism of the Spirit. The One to whom he pointed would perform this Spirit baptism. When God sent His Spirit at Pentecost, He inaugurated an age when the risen Lord continued His work in His people through His Spirit.

3. Baptism of Jesus (1:9–11)

9 And it came to pass in those days, that Jesus came from Nazareth [NAZ uhr reth] of Galilee [GAL ih lee], and was baptized of John in Jordan.

10 And straightway coming up out of the water, he saw the heavens opened, and the Spirit like a dove descending upon him:

11 And there came a voice from heaven, saying, Thou art my beloved Son, in whom I am well pleased.

Jesus prepared to launch His own ministry by coming to John for baptism. He obviously had no sins to confess, so why did He come? He came to identify with the sinners He had come to save and to picture His coming death and resurrection. The words from heaven echo Psalm 2:7 and Isaiah 42:1. One of these declares the Messiah to be the Son of God; the other shows that the Son of God would fulfill His mission as the Servant who suffers.

This is one of the Bible passages that depicts God the Father, God the Son, and God the Holy Spirit. One God has revealed Himself as Father, Son, and Spirit. The doctrine of the Trinity remains a mystery, but it matches the revelation of the Scriptures and our own experiences. We know God as Creator and Father to whom we pray; as Son who lived, died, and was raised for our salvation; and as Spirit who is with us and among us.

4. Temptations of Jesus (1:12–13)

Mark does not describe the temptations as Matthew (4:1–11) and Luke (4:1–13) do. He tells us that the Spirit drove Jesus into the wilderness, where He was tempted by Satan, after which the angels ministered to Him.

5. Jesus preaching the gospel (1:14–15)

14 Now after that John was put in prison, Jesus came into Galilee, preaching the gospel of the kingdom of God,

15 And saying, The time is fulfilled, and the kingdom of God is at hand: repent ye, and believe the gospel.

Mark 6:14–29 tells about John's arrest, imprisonment, and execution. Herod Antipas arrested John because the bold preacher had denounced Herod and Herodias for their immoral marriage. Mark 1:14 says that Jesus launched His ministry after John was arrested. John was the forerunner of Jesus by his preaching and also by his suffering and death. Jesus too would be arrested and killed, but His death would atone for the sins of the world.

Mark 1:15 gives us the gist of what Jesus preached. He preached that the decisive time in God's redemptive plan had arrived. God's time was fulfilled. His reign was to be declared and offered to all people. Jesus' life, death, and resurrection were the heart of God's saving work. The future for which we hope is rooted in what God has already done in history through His Son, our Savior.

As John had called people to repent in preparation for the Coming One, Jesus called people to repent and believe because He was that One. Repentance and faith describe the human response to God's grace in Christ. These represent two sides of the same thing. *Repent* means to turn from sin, and *believe* means to turn to the Lord (see Acts 20:21).

II. When John Was in Prison (Luke 7:18–30)

1. John's question (7:18–20)

18 And the disciples of John shewed him of all these things.

Luke 7:18–30 took place some time after John was imprisoned. While he was there, Jesus was engaged in His ministry of preaching, healing, and helping. John had loyal followers who served as his disciples. They reported to John what Jesus was doing. "These things" refers to things like those recorded in Luke 7:1–17: healing the centurion's servant and restoring to life the son of the widow of Nain.

19 And John calling unto him two of his disciples sent them to Jesus, saying, Art thou he that should come? or look we for another?

20 When the men were come unto him, they said, John the Baptist hath sent us unto thee, saying, Art thou he that should come? or look we for another?

Why would John, who had so boldly preached Jesus as the Messiah, ask such a question? John seems to have been puzzled by the kind of ministry Jesus was performing. John had pictured the Messiah vindicating the righteous and punishing the wicked (Luke 3:17). Instead a righteous man like John languished in prison while the evil Herod and Herodias lived in luxury and security. Meanwhile Jesus was quietly going about helping needy people. John was puzzled because Jesus' actions did not match John's expectations.

2. Jesus' answer (7:21–23)

21 And in that same hour he cured many of their infirmities and plagues, and of evil spirits; and unto many that were blind he gave sight.

22 Then Jesus answering said unto them, Go your way, and tell John what things ye have seen and heard; how that the blind see, the lame walk, the lepers are cleansed, the deaf hear, the dead are raised, to the poor the gospel is preached.

23 And blessed is he, whosoever shall not be offended in me.

John dealt with his perplexity in the way people of faith deal with their doubts and questions. He addressed his question to Jesus. The Lord's answer was to tell John's disciples to report to John what Jesus was doing. Jesus was performing the kind of ministry predicted of the Servant in Isaiah. He had not come to bring final judgment but to make salvation possible.

When Jesus spoke in the synagogue in Nazareth, He read Isaiah 61:1–2 (see Luke 4:18–19). Using almost the same words, Jesus reminded John of His ministry of helping, healing, and preaching good news to the poor. John knew the Scriptures; Jesus expected John to recognize His actions as fulfillment of Scripture. John was not the only one close to Jesus who misunderstood His mission. Even the disciples of Jesus did not understand until after the Crucifixion and Resurrection.

3. Jesus' commendation of John (7:24–30)

Jesus used the occasion to commend John before the people. He did not want anyone to think He was being critical of John. Jesus reminded the people that they had not gone to the wilderness to see a timid person, like a reed blown about by the wind (v. 24). They had not gone to see pampered, well-dressed royalty (v. 25). Instead they had gone to see a man who was a prophet, indeed more than a prophet (v. 26). John was the messenger of the Lord foretold in Malachi 3:1 (v. 27). Jesus spoke the enigmatic words of verse 28 about none being greater than John, but the least in the kingdom being greater than he (v. 28). John was the last and greatest of the prophets, but he did not live to see the fulfillment of Christ's mission. Those who had listened to John praised God (v. 29), but the religious leaders rejected what God was doing through John and Jesus (v. 30).

APPLYING THE BIBLE

1. Sam Houston's baptism. Sam Houston played a key role in Texas's fight for independence from Mexico. He was the first president of the Republic of Texas. After Texas joined the Union, he served as governor and United States Senator.

When Lyndon B. Johnson was president, there hung on his wall a framed letter from Houston to Johnson's great-grandfather preacher who had led Houston to Christ. When Houston was converted he was a changed man. On the day he was baptized; he was reminded that his wallet was in his pocket. His reply was he wanted that baptized too!

A great many converts have been baptized; but, apparently, they left their purses high and dry as attested to by their giving records!

2. A great baptismal service. Were you baptized out-of-doors in a creek or a lake? Many have witnessed such moving services with the crowd lining the banks and the new converts making a long line down to the water, waiting their turn to follow the Lord in baptism.

John's baptism was a great one as multitudes came from all over Judea to be baptized in the Jordan River. Indeed, it was a happy day (Mark 1:5).

3. John's preaching. John's preaching included both a warning and a proclamation. He warned sinners to repent and confess their sins for the remission of sins (Mark 1:4), and demonstrate their change of heart by baptism (v.5). The joyous proclamation was that One was coming who would baptize them in the Holy Spirit (vv.7–8). In his desert preaching, John was preparing the way for Jesus to begin His public ministry.

Preaching today must also emphasize these same elements: repentance from sin, confession of sin, baptism, and the good news that Christ can change lives.

4. True humility. Abraham Lincoln was truly a humble man. But aren't the truly great men and women of history marked by this characteristic?

On one occasion, Lincoln called at General McClellan's house but was told the general had gone to a reception. Lincoln waited and waited, and finally the general returned home. Although he was told the president was waiting, McClellan ascended the stairs and went to bed. When the message was given to Lincoln, he quietly left. Later, Lincoln appointed McClellan as head of the Union Army. When Lincoln was asked by friends why he tolerated McClellan's insolence, the President replied: "Why, I would be willing to hold McClellan's horse, if only he will give victory to our army."

True humility was also one of John's chief virtues. He told his hearers that the One coming was mightier than he; that he was not worthy to stoop down and unlatch Jesus' sandals; that he must decrease but that Jesus must increase; and that he needed to be baptized of Jesus rather than baptize Jesus himself.

Unlike many of us who are offended at the least affront, there was none of this in John. He gave himself away in order to serve his Lord.

5. Satan's choice tool. Perhaps doubt is Satan's favorite tool. If he can get us to doubt our salvation or the goodness of God, he can destroy our Christian usefulness.

John the Baptist, suffering in prison, was plagued by deep doubts about the authenticity of Jesus (Luke 7:19–20). Jesus gave John the answer he needed for assurance (vv. 22–23). Satan is the author of doubt! Doubt no more about your relationship to Jesus. Do what John did: take it to Jesus and leave it there!

TEACHING THE BIBLE

▶ *Main Idea:* When we have doubts about Jesus, we should take them directly to Him.

▶ *Suggested Teaching Aim:* To lead adults to express their doubts to Jesus.

A TEACHING OUTLINE

1. Use a unit poster and an illustration to introduce the Bible study.

2. Use an advanced assignment to involve a member and enhance the lesson.

3. Use a poster and group discussion to guide Bible study.

4. Use group discussion to give the truth a personal focus.

Introduce the Bible Study

Prepare and display the following unit poster for the next four Sundays. Mark the lesson being studied each week.

Persons in Jesus' Ministry

John the Baptizer (Mark 1:1–15; Luke 7:18–30)—January 5
Mary and Martha (Luke 10:38–42; John 12:1–8)—January 12
Peter (Matt. 4:18–20; 16:13–23)—January 19
Judas Iscariot (Matt. 26:14–16, 20–25, 47–50; 27:1–5)—January 26

Ask: Is it wrong to question God? Say: Most of the great characters of the Bible questioned God. The lesson today is about one of these. Point out the theme for the next four Sundays and highlight the lesson for today.

Search for Biblical Truth

IN ADVANCE, enlist a member to read about "John the Baptist," in the *Holman Bible Dictionary,* page 805, or that entry in some other Bible dictionary and present a two- to three-minute report. On a chalkboard or a large sheet of paper write, "The Gospel and John's Ministry." Ask a volunteer to read Mark 1:4–6. Use a map of Judea to point out the Jordan River near Jericho as a possible site for John's preaching and baptizing. Ask: In what two actions did John engage? (Preaching and baptizing.) Ask a volunteer to read Luke 3:7–14 as an example of John's preaching. Ask members to identify elements in John's preaching. (Turn from sins, do right, be baptized.) Use "Studying the Bible" to explain the source of his baptism.

Write "John and the One Mightier than He" on the chalkboard. Use "True Humility" from "Applying the Bible." Ask: How did John demonstrate his true humility? (Said he was not worthy even to untie the Messiah's shoes.) How did John say his baptism differed from Jesus' baptism? (John's was water baptism; Jesus' was Spirit baptism.)

Write "Baptism of Jesus" on the chalkboard. Ask: Why did Jesus ask John to baptize Him? (See "Studying the Bible" for answers.) How does this passage depict the Trinity? (Father—spoke; Spirit—descended like a dove; Son—baptized.)

Ask a volunteer to read 1:14–15. Summarize the material in Mark 6:14–29 to explain why John was put in prison. Ask: What was the basic content of Jesus' preaching? (See v. 15.) IN ADVANCE, write this sentence from "Studying the Bible" on a sheet of paper and place on the focal wall: "Repent means to turn from sin, and believe means to turn to the Lord."

Write "John's Question" on the chalkboard. Call for a volunteer to read Luke 7:18–20. Ask: Why do you think John questioned whether Jesus was the Messiah? (See "Studying the Bible" for possible answers.)

Write "Jesus' Answer" on the chalkboard. Ask: What do you think of Jesus' answer to John's question as to whether He was the Messiah? Did Jesus really answer John's question? Do you think this answer satisfied John?

Give the Truth a Personal Focus

Ask: What do you do when you have doubts about God? Ask members to identify the process John followed. (Questioned, expressed his questions, went to Jesus for answers.) Say: Doubts are only wrong when we fail to bring them to Jesus. Jesus may not always answer our questions in the direct way we want; but if we are honest in asking, He will be honest in responding. Encourage members to express their doubts to Jesus and to be willing to seek Jesus' answer.

Mary and Martha

Basic Passages: Luke 10:38–42; John 12:1–8

Focal Passages: Luke 10:38–42; John 12:1–8

Mary and Martha were among the larger group of Jesus' friends and followers. They did not follow Jesus on His travels as did the apostles and some other followers, including some women (Luke 8:1–3). Instead, they showed their loyalty by what they did in a home setting. Martha exercised the gift of hospitality, and Mary sat at Jesus' feet to learn. She also showed great love and understanding as Jesus neared the time of His death.

▶**Study Aim:** *To explain what the words and actions of Mary, Martha, and Jesus reveal about Mary and Martha*

STUDYING THE BIBLE

OUTLINE AND SUMMARY

I. **Jesus in the Home of Mary and Martha (Luke 10:38–42)**

   1. Two sisters (10:38–39)

   2. Martha's complaint (10:40)

   3. Jesus' reply to Martha (10:41–42)

II. **Mary Anointing Jesus (John 12:1–8)**

   1. After the raising of Lazarus from the dead (12:1–2)

   2. Mary's actions (12:3)

   3. Judas's objections (12:4–6)

   4. Jesus' defense of Mary (12:7–8)

Martha received Jesus into her home, and her sister Mary sat at His feet and heard His words (Luke 10:38–39). Martha asked Jesus if He didn't care that Mary had left her to do all the work; she also asked Jesus to tell Mary to help (Luke 10:40). Jesus told Martha that she was anxious about many things while Mary had chosen the one thing that is necessary (Luke 10:41–42). After Jesus had raised Lazarus (LAZ uh ruhs) from the dead, He went to a meal where Martha served and Lazarus was at the table (John 12:1–2). Mary anointed Jesus' feet with expensive ointment and wiped His feet with her hair (John 12:3). Judas, treasurer for Jesus and the twelve, asked why the money had not been used to help the poor; but his motive was not concern, but greed (John 12:5–6). After Jesus told Judas to leave Mary alone, He commended her for anointing Him for burial, adding that—in contrast to helping the poor—anointing His body was a unique opportunity (John 12:7–8).

I. Jesus in the Home of Mary and Martha (Luke 10:38–42)

1. Two sisters (10:38–39)

38 Now it came to pass, as they went, that he entered into a certain village: and a certain woman named Martha received him into her house.

39 And she had a sister called Mary, which also sat at Jesus' feet, and heard his word.

John tells us that Mary and Martha lived in the village of Bethany (BETH uh nih) with their brother Lazarus (John 11:1). Bethany was about two miles southeast of Jerusalem (John 11:18). The last part of verse 38 evidently means that Martha was the mistress of the house and probably the older sister.

Martha showed her hospitality by greeting Jesus and welcoming Him into her house. Mary showed her devotion by sitting at Jesus' feet to learn from Him. "Sitting at someone's feet" was a way of saying that the person was studying under that teacher. The tense of the verb "heard" shows that Mary was continuing to listen to Jesus. Since rabbis did not teach women, Jesus having Mary as a student was a revolutionary act for both Mary and Jesus.

2. Martha's complaint (10:40)

40 But Martha was cumbered about much serving, and came to him, and said, Lord, dost thou not care that my sister hath left me to serve alone? bid her therefore that she help me.

The word "cumbered" means to be drawn about in different directions. She was distracted by her many duties in preparing the meal for Jesus. Every hostess can sympathize with what Martha was feeling. She had more to do than she had time to do it unless Mary joined in the preparations, but Mary seemed blissfully unaware of Martha's frustration. Finally her frustration became so great that she said something about it. However, rather than speaking directly to her sister, Martha addressed her complaint to Jesus. She asked a question and she made a request.

The question shows that she was not only angry with Mary, but she also was peeved with Jesus. Martha asked Jesus if He didn't care that Mary had left her to do all the work alone. This was a bold and brash thing for a hostess to say to any guest, especially to a rabbi, and even more especially to Jesus. However, Martha was so frustrated by all she had to do that she spoke in the heat of the moment. Later, she probably regretted such rash words. Jesus always cares for people, even if it appears to us that He doesn't.

Martha also asked Jesus to tell Mary to help her sister prepare the meal for their guest. Martha probably felt that Mary would pay no attention to Martha if Martha asked her to help. However, if their respected guest asked Mary to help, Martha felt that her sister would obey.

3. Jesus' reply to Martha (10:41–42)

41 And Jesus answered and said unto her, Martha, Martha, thou art careful and troubled about many things:

42 But one thing is needful: and Mary hath chosen that good part, which shall not be taken away from her.

The word "care" in verse 40 and the word "careful" in verse 41 are different words. The word Jesus used in verse 41 is the same word He used in warning against worldly anxiety (see Matt. 6:25, 28, 31, 34; Luke 12:11, 22, 26). The word implies a division and distraction of one's thoughts and actions based on a concern for too many material things. Martha was anxious and distracted about many things: about the many dishes she needed to prepare and having the table and room just right.

Jesus told Martha that only one thing is necessary in the long run— hearing and responding to the word of God. Mary had chosen to spend this precious time sitting at the feet of Jesus. By so choosing, she had chosen something that nothing would ever take away from her.

The words of Jesus should not be taken as diminishing the value of Christian hospitality. Feeding and caring for others in one's home is clearly taught in the Bible. Hebrews 13:2 calls for believers to show hospitality to strangers as well as friends, "for thereby some have entertained angels unawares." This verse had in mind the warm welcome given by Abraham and Sarah to the three men who came to their tent, three men who later turned out to be two angels and the Lord (Gen. 18). Thus Martha felt she was showing that kind of hospitality to Jesus.

Some of life's choices are between good and bad, but many choices are between good and best. Martha's hospitality was good, but she was missing the best: to sit at Jesus' feet. Jesus' words were repeating the teaching that "man shall not live by bread alone, but by every word of God" (Luke 4:4; see Deut. 8:3). He was also restating what He said in Matthew 6:25–34. After warning against anxiety about food and clothing, Jesus said, "Seek ye first the kingdom of God, and his righteousness; and all these things shall be added unto you" (Matt. 6:33). Martha was concerned about a lavish meal in which everything was just right. Jesus would have preferred simple fare that would have allowed Martha to spend more time with Him.

II. Mary Anointing Jesus (John 12:1–8)

1. After the raising of Lazarus from the dead (12:1–2)

1 Then Jesus six days before the passover came to Bethany, where Lazarus was which had been dead, whom he raised from the dead.

2 There they made him a supper; and Martha served: but Lazarus was one of them that sat at the table with him.

Review John 11 to see the dramatic account of Jesus raising Lazarus from the dead. After that great miracle, the enemies of Jesus decided that Jesus must be killed (John 11:53). In this atmosphere, Jesus came to Bethany only a few days before His death. Jesus was invited to a supper. Mark 14:3 and Matthew 26:6 say that the meal was served in the house of Simon the leper. Martha was in her usual role as the one who served the meal. Lazarus was one of those at the meal.

2. Mary's actions (12:3)

3 Then took Mary a pound of ointment of spikenard, very costly, and anointed the feet of Jesus, and wiped his feet with her hair: and the house was filled with the odour of the ointment.

Spikenard was an expensive ointment or perfume. The heads of kings were often anointed with something like this (1 Sam. 10:1). Mary anointed the feet of Jesus with an entire pound of this ointment. This was a very expensive gift. Judas later estimated the cost as being about three hundred pence or denarii. Since a denarius was what a laborer earned for a day's work (Matt. 20:2), three hundred denarii were about a year's salary of a laborer, a considerable amount of money.

The humblest parts of the body were the feet. The crowning glory of a woman was her long hair (1 Cor. 11:15). It was unthinkable for a woman of Mary's reputation to use her hair to wipe someone's feet. The act showed Mary's humility and great love and devotion for Jesus. The Lord Himself also saw it as an act that encouraged Him as He faced the cross (vv. 7–8).

3. Judas's objections (12:4–6)

4 Then saith one of his disciples, Judas Iscariot, Simon's son, which should betray him,

5 Why was not this ointment sold for three hundred pence, and given to the poor?

6 This he said, not that he cared for the poor; but because he was a thief, and had the bag, and bare what was put therein.

We are not told to whom Judas addressed his question. Everyone no doubt heard it, including Mary. His words were actually an accusation against Mary. He was saying that she was wasteful and callous toward the poor. If the expensive ointment had been sold, the money could have fed many poor people.

Because Judas served as treasurer for Jesus and the apostles, he apparently felt it was his place to lodge this objection. Looking back at the words of Judas, who later betrayed Jesus, John wrote that Judas did not speak because he cared for the poor. Instead he cared for himself. John tells us that Judas was a thief who took for himself some of the money of Jesus and the others.

4. Jesus' defense of Mary (12:7–8)

7 Then said Jesus, Let her alone: against the day of my burying hath she kept this.

8 For the poor always ye have with you; but me ye have not always.

Rather than agreeing with Judas, Jesus sharply rebuked him. Jesus knew that the words of Judas must have cut Mary to the quick. Therefore, as Judas had publicly questioned Mary's act, Jesus publicly told Judas to leave Mary alone. Then He said that her act showed an empathy about His coming death and burial. She anointed Him ahead of time.

Jesus was only a few days away from His death. He had tried to tell His followers about His coming rejection, suffering, death, and resurrection; however, most of them had not understood. For the Messiah to suffer was too different from what they expected Him to do. As the end drew near, two of His followers seem to have taken Jesus seriously about His coming death. One was Mary of Bethany, and the other was Judas. They responded very differently to their awareness of Jesus' coming death. Judas betrayed Him, but Mary anointed Him as if for burial. Her act meant much to Jesus because it showed that at least one of His friends empathized with what He was going through.

Verse 8 has sometimes been understood to teach a callous acceptance of the plight of the poor. That was not Jesus' point. We know that He cared for the poor because of His own actions and teachings (Matt. 25:34–40; Luke 14:13, 21). Under the leadership of the Spirit of the Lord, the early Christians often showed their love for the poor (Acts 4:34–35; Rom. 15:26; Gal. 2:10; James 1:27–2:6, 14–16; 1 John 3:16–18).

APPLYING THE BIBLE

1. The epitaph on David Livingstone's parents' tombstone. David Livingstone, a pioneer missionary to Africa, wrote the epitaph that appears on his parents' headstone at Blantyre, Scotland: "To show the resting place of Neil Livingstone and Agnes Hunter, his wife, and to express the thankfulness of their children . . . for poor and pious parents."

Whether they are rich or poor parents is immaterial. But blessed are the children who are reared by pious parents—though it may take a lifetime for the children to recognize it.

Martha and Mary were not poor by the standards of their day but they were pious, each expressing her love for Jesus in her own way (Luke 10:38–39).

2. Angry Martha. Frustrated with all she had to do, Martha blurted out her anger (v. 40). Martha was also peeved at Jesus because Mary was sitting at His feet and He seemed not to care that Martha had all the work to do (v. 40). Notice that she did not take her complaint directly to Mary but went around her to Jesus. That's no way to confront people with whom we have difficulties. They need to be confronted directly but kindly. Telling loved ones and friends about the problem only fans a small fire into a bigger one.

When the British attacked New Orleans during the War of 1812, Andrew Jackson, who later became the seventh President of the United States, stopped the British cannonballs with bales of cotton. The soft cotton, crushed into strong bales, was a good defense. Solomon says the same kind of defense will work with people who irritate or anger us: "A soft answer turneth away wrath: but grievous words stir up anger" (Prov. 15:1). Look at how gently Jesus handled Martha's anger (Luke 10:41–42). What an example for us to follow. Almost everyone will respond to kindness and a smile.

3. Each of us can serve Jesus. In one way or another, each of us can serve Jesus. There are no believers without talents to dedicate to the

Lord. Sure, some have one talent while others have two or ten. But each of us is endowed with some gift of service and love to give the Master. Mary was quiet and introspective, while Martha was outgoing, outspoken, and an activist. Mary sat at His feet and listened (v. 39), while Martha worked and served (v. 40, John 12:2). Probably Mary was no cook, and Martha was too active to sit still. Mary chose the better part, Jesus said (Luke 10:42), and He told Martha she was too "careful and troubled about many things" (v. 41). But He didn't condemn Martha for doing what she could. It takes both the Marys and Marthas to do the work of God.

4. Lazarus at the table. How would you feel to sit down by and visit with someone who had died and come back? In the dinner that Mary and Martha gave, there were two outstanding attractions—Lazarus and Jesus (John 12:1–2). Either would have attracted a crowd: Lazarus who was raised from the dead (11:38–44); and Jesus who had raised Lazarus. What a day in Bethany!

5. Humble extravagance. On the humblest part of the body, the feet, Mary poured her most extravagant gift, the spikenard, and dried Jesus' feet with her long hair, her crowning glory. What humble extravagance. Jesus was worthy of the best Mary had.

What a moving thing it is to read about someone who is extremely wealthy giving millions of dollars to the Lord's work. But that kind of gift given out of one's wealth counts no more with Jesus—though it makes the headlines—than the sacrificial gift given out of one's poverty (Mark 12:41–44). Christ accepts and honors all gifts given to Him, but the sacrificial gift is honored more (Mark 12:43). It is the spirit of giving that counts most.

6. Greed. Money is not evil, but the love of money is (1 Tim. 6:10). Greed, not concern for the poor, was Judas's problem (John 12:4–6). An anonymous poet expressed Judas's greed like this:

> Dug from the mountain side or washed in the glen,
> Servant am I or the master of men.
> Earn me, I bless you; steal me, I curse you.
> Grasp me and hold me—a fiend shall possess you.
> Lie for me, die for me; covet me; take me.
> Angel or devil, I am what you make me.

TEACHING THE BIBLE

▶ *Main Idea:* We can only serve Jesus when we serve Him the way He wants to be served.

▶ *Suggested Teaching Aim:* To lead adults to determine a selfless act they will perform for Jesus.

A TEACHING OUTLINE

1. Use a question to introduce the Bible study.
2. Enlist a member to read the Scripture.

3. Use a poster to identify Mary and Martha.
4. Use discussion questions to guide the Bible study.
5. Use discussion questions to apply the study.

Introduce the Bible Study

Ask: What is the most selfless act you have seen performed? Allow responses. Ask: What is the most selfless act you have performed? (Do not allow responses.) Use the unit poster prepared last week to indicate the lesson for today and point out that Mary performed a loving, selfless act commended by Jesus.

Search for Biblical Truth

Use a map to locate Bethany about two miles southeast of Jerusalem. On a chalkboard or a large sheet of paper write *Martha* and *Mary* at the top of two columns. Ask members to share what they know about these two and write their responses under each heading.

IN ADVANCE, enlist a reader for all of the Scripture. Call for the reader to read Luke 10:38–40. Ask: Why do you think Martha was upset? Since Mary was doing something that only men did in the first century, do you think Martha was upset by Mary's boldness? Why do you think Mary did not help Martha? Which one of these two women can you identify with most? Have you ever been angry with Jesus?

Ask the reader to read Luke 10:41–42. Ask: Did Martha have a responsibility and a right as mistress of the house to be concerned about preparing the meal? Was Martha doing what Jesus wanted done or what she wanted to do for Jesus? How do you reconcile Jesus' words here with the command for Christian hospitality in Hebrews 13:2? What is the most important thing as far as Jesus was concerned? Have you ever done what you wanted to do for Jesus instead of what He wanted you to do for Him?

Call for the reader to read John 12:1–3. Ask: Do you think Martha approached this meal any differently than she did the earlier one? How about Mary? How long does it take you to learn lessons Jesus wants to teach?

Call for the reader to read John 12:4–3. Use "Studying the Bible" to explain Mary's act and its value. Say: One way of looking at the value of her gift is that working forty hours a week at $5.00 an hour for a year would be $10,400. Mary's gift was quite expensive. Ask: How do you think Jesus felt when Mary anointed His feet? How do you think Mary felt? Why do you think she did it? Do you think she had planned it?

Call for the reader to read John 12:4–8. Ask: If you had been present, how would you have felt when Mary anointed Jesus? What was Judas's concern? How did Jesus interpret her action? How do you think Judas felt when Jesus rebuked him? How do you feel when someone rebukes you in front of people whose opinions you value? How do you think Mary felt about Judas's comments? Why do you think Mary's act meant so much to Jesus? How do you feel when you do something out of love and someone interprets it differently?

Give the Truth a Personal Focus

Ask: Can Christians be wasteful when it comes to giving to Jesus? Without responding aloud, what have you done in a spontaneous way that demonstrated great love for Jesus? How did you feel? Have you felt like you should do something loving and spontaneous but refused? How did you feel?

Challenge members to think of one act of love they will perform for Jesus just because they love Him and for no other reason. Allow time for private prayer and thought. Then close in prayer that members will have the courage to follow through on their decisions.

Peter

Basic Passages: Matthew 4:18–20; 16:13–23

Focal Passages: Matthew 4:18–20; 16:13–23

Many Christians can identify with Simon Peter. He had high moments when he said and did inspiring things. At other times, he said and did things that showed his frailty and humanity. The Bible passages for this lesson include both kinds of words by Peter.

▶**Study Aim:** *To explain Peter's confession and rebuke of Jesus and the response Jesus made to each*

STUDYING THE BIBLE

OUTLINE AND SUMMARY
    I. Following Jesus (Matt. 4:18–20)
    II. Confessing Jesus as the Messiah (Matt. 16:13–23)
       1. Peter confesses Jesus as the Christ (16:13–16)
       2. Jesus commends Peter (16:17–19)
       3. Jesus predicts His own death (16:20–21)
       4. Jesus rebukes Peter (16:22–23)

When Jesus called Peter to follow Him, Peter immediately did so (4:18–20). Although many thought of Jesus as a prophet, Peter confessed Him as the Messiah (16:13–16). Jesus blessed Peter and promised to build His church that death could not destroy (16:17–19). After warning Peter not to tell anyone He was the Messiah, Jesus predicted His death and resurrection (16:20–21). Peter rebuked Jesus for saying such a thing, and Jesus rebuked Peter for becoming an instrument of Satan (16:22–23).

I. Following Jesus (Matt. 4:18–20)

18 And Jesus, walking by the sea of Galilee [GAL ih lee], saw two brethren, Simon called Peter, and Andrew his brother, casting a net into the sea: for they were fishers.

19 And he saith unto them, Follow me, and I will make you fishers of men.

20 And they straightway left their nets, and followed him.

Peter and Andrew were fishers by trade. Jesus sought them out while they were at work. When Jesus used the words "follow me," He was calling people to make a commitment to Him that superseded other commitments (Luke 9:57–62). The follower was to be with Jesus, learn from Him, be loyal to Him, and help Him fulfill His mission. Thus Jesus called Peter and Andrew to become fishers of men. The words "follow me" were used by Jesus to call people to become His disciples. The word "disciples" is often used of the Twelve who became the closest followers of Jesus (Matt. 10:1); however, the word was also used to describe the larger group of followers (Matt. 8:21).

John 1:35–42 records an earlier encounter of Jesus with these two brothers. Andrew had been a disciple of John the Baptist. When John had pointed to Jesus as the Lamb of God, Andrew told Simon about Jesus. When Simon came to investigate, Jesus said, "Thou art Simon the son of Jona: thou shalt be called Cephas [SEE fuhs], which is by interpretation, A stone" (John 1:42). "Cephas" is the Aramaic (air uh MAY ick) word for "stone." Although Andrew first brought Peter to Jesus, Peter became more prominent. In the lists of the Twelve, Peter's name is listed first. In verse 18, Peter is listed before Andrew.

II. Confessing Jesus as the Messiah (Matt. 16:13–23)

1. Peter confesses Jesus as the Christ (16:13–16)

13 When Jesus came into the coasts of Caesarea [ses uh REE uh] Philippi [FIL uh pigh], he asked his disciples, saying Whom do men say that I the Son of man am?

14 And they said, Some say that thou art John the Baptist: some, Elias [ih LIGH uhs]; and others Jeremias [jer ih MIGHS uhs], or one of the prophets.

Caesarea Philippi was a town located about twenty-five miles north of the Sea of Galilee (GAL ih lee). Herod Philip had named it for himself and Tiberias (tigh BIR ih uhs) Caesar (SEE zur). The word "coasts" does not mean sea coast, but a region or part of the country.

Before asking His disciples their own opinion of Him, Jesus first asked them what others were saying about who He was. Jesus referred to Himself as Son of man, the title Jesus most often used of Himself. After John the

A very calm Sea of Galilee at dusk in northern Israel as viewed from the southwestern shoreline towards snow-capped Mt. Hermon to the northeast. Credit: Biblical Illustrator.

Baptist had been executed, some people thought that Jesus was John the Baptist raised from the dead (Matt. 14:1–2). Because Malachi 4:5–6 predicted that Elijah would precede the coming of the Lord, some people thought Jesus was Elijah. Others thought Jesus was Jeremiah or one of the other prophets.

15 He saith unto them, But whom say ye that I am?

16 And Simon Peter answered and said, Thou art the Christ, the Son of the living God.

Jesus asked the disciples who they thought He was. Notice that "ye" is plural. He addressed His question to all the disciples; but as was often the case, Peter was the one who answered. He often served as spokesman for the group. At other times, he simply was the first to speak.

Peter used two titles to describe who he thought Jesus was. "Christ" is the Greek equivalent of "Messiah." Both words mean "anointed one." Since kings were often anointed, the word had come to mean "king." God had promised David that a descendant of his would reign over an everlasting kingdom (2 Sam. 7:13–16). For centuries, Jews had looked for the coming of this Messiah. Peter's confession shows that he believed that Jesus was the promised Messiah.

Peter also called Jesus "the Son of the living God." The angel Gabriel had used the same title to describe Jesus when Gabriel told the virgin Mary that she was to have a son, who would be conceived by the Holy Spirit (Luke 1:35). At the baptism of Jesus, God's voice from heaven had declared that Jesus was His beloved Son (Matt. 3:17).

2. Jesus commends Peter (16:17–19)

17 And Jesus answered and said unto him, Blessed art thou, Simon Bar-jona [bahr-JOH nuh]: for flesh and blood hath not revealed it unto thee, but my Father which is in heaven.

In pronouncing a blessing on Peter, Jesus said that this faith of Peter's was not a purely human achievement. Peter had not reasoned his way to this conclusion. God had used the words and acts of Jesus to reveal to Peter that Jesus was His Son and the promised Messiah.

18 And I say also unto thee, That thou art Peter, and upon this rock I will build my church; and the gates of hell shall not prevail against it.

Verse 18 has been one of the most controversial verses in Christian history. The controversy swirls about the meaning of the words "this rock." Various Bible students have identified the rock as Christ, as Peter, as Peter's confession of faith, or as a combination of the above. Christ Himself is surely the ultimate foundation of the church (1 Cor. 3:11). On the other hand, the apostles can also be referred to as the foundation of the church (Eph. 2:20; Rev. 21:14). The testimony of the apostles, the unique eyewitnesses of Jesus, in a sense forms the foundation for the church.

If Jesus was referring to Peter as the rock, He may have seen him as representing all the apostles, whose testimony would provide the church's foundation. If Jesus was speaking of Peter himself, He was thinking of Peter's leadership role among the disciples and in the early church. Only one group sees this verse as justification for claiming Peter as the first pope and the head of a worldwide organization, controlled by Peter's successors.

When Christ spoke of "my church," He was speaking of His people, not an organization. Most of the uses of the word "church" in the New Testament refer to local congregations of believers. See, for example, Matthew 18:17. However, in Matthew 16:18, He was referring to those who, like Peter, confess Him as Christ and Son of God. He calls such to follow Him and be His people.

The phrase "the gates of hell [*hades*]" was often used to mean "the power of death." Thus the promise is that the power of death will not be able to destroy Christ's church. Christ was soon to die, and many of His followers would be put to death; but death would not be able to overcome the church.

19 And I will give unto thee the keys of the kingdom of heaven: and whatsoever thou shalt bind on earth shall be bound in heaven: and whatsoever thou shalt loose on earth shall be loosed in heaven.

Those who see Peter as the first pope of a universal church organization interpret verse 19 as the church's power to forgive sins. Whatever Jesus meant, He later said similar words to the church (Matt. 18:18). Jesus' image of keys of the kingdom may refer to the church's responsibility to make entrance to the kingdom available to people by telling them of Christ. The Lord is the One who receives people into His kingdom, but He has entrusted to us the task of pointing people to the open door. When we fail in our task, we in essence close the door to the kingdom to those who need our witness.

3. Jesus predicts His death (16:20–21)

20 Then charged he his disciples that they should tell no man that he was Jesus the Christ.

21 From that time forth began Jesus to shew unto his disciples, how that he must go unto Jerusalem, and suffer many things of the elders and chief priests and scribes, and be killed, and be raised again the third day.

Why would Jesus commend Peter for confessing Him as Christ and then command Peter and the others not to tell anyone? A study of the Gospels shows that Jesus was reluctant to use the title Messiah of Himself. He knew that many Jews were looking for an earthly king who would lead Israel to defeat the Romans and to make the people prosper. After Jesus fed the five thousand, some tried to make Him their king; but He refused (John 6:15). Therefore, Jesus warned Peter and the others not yet to tell others that Jesus was the Messiah. After His death and resurrection, He would commission them to tell the whole world (Matt. 28:18–20).

Jesus knew that the disciples themselves shared the false expectations of the people about the Messiah. Therefore, after commending Peter for his confession, Jesus began to teach His followers the kind of Messiah He had come to be. He told them that He must go to Jerusalem, where He would suffer many things at the hands of the religious leaders. Jesus predicted that He would be killed, but be raised again on the third day.

It was as if Jesus said to Peter: "You are right about me being the Messiah, but let me explain to you the kind of Messiah I am. I am not going to lead an army or use my powers to build an earthly kingdom. To the contrary, I am going to be rejected, to suffer and die, and to be raised from the dead. Only in that way will I be able to save people from sin and death, and thus to fulfill my Father's mission for Me."

4. Jesus rebukes Peter (16:22–23)

22 Then Peter took him, and began to rebuke him, saying, Be it far from thee, Lord: this shall not be unto thee.

23 But he turned, and said unto Peter, Get thee behind me, Satan: thou art an offence unto me: for thou savorest not the things that be of God, but those that be of men.

One minute Peter was confessing Jesus as the Christ. The next minute Peter was rebuking Jesus for speaking of His suffering and death. Peter obviously shared the popular view of the Messiah. Although he had come to believe that Jesus was the promised Messiah, he never expected the Messiah to suffer and die. In the popular view, the Messiah was a warrior king like his forefather David. The last thing such a king would do would be to allow himself to suffer and be killed.

Just as Peter used forceful language to rebuke Jesus, so did Jesus in rebuking Peter. Earlier Peter had spoken what God had revealed to him. Now he spoke words that grew out of human understanding, not divine revelation. Jesus had just commended Peter as a rock, but now he was becoming a stumbling block ("offence"). Peter's words constituted a recurrence of the temptations of Satan for Jesus to find some other way than the cross to achieve His purpose (Matt. 4:1–11).

APPLYING THE BIBLE

1. Building up God's kingdom. How does God build His kingdom? By one poor, hungry beggar telling another where to find the Bread of Life.

As our lesson points out, Andrew had found the Messiah (John 1:35–42) and he introduced Peter, his brother, to Jesus. In his book *God's Psychiatry*, Charles Allen observes that in a year if one person brought another person to Jesus, at the end of the year there would be two believers. Following that same pattern, at the end of the second year there would be four believers. And now for the shocker! At the end of just thirty-one years, one winning one, there would be 2,147,483,648 believers! Since Jesus died for us nearly two thousand years ago, we have had enough time to win hundreds of worlds like ours. We haven't done it because we have not been faithful followers of Him whom we call Lord and Master.

2. Hand-picked fruit. John Bunyan, author of *Pilgrim's Progress,* was won to Jesus as he overheard three women talking about the joy they had in Christ. William Carey, the father of the modern missionary movement, was led to Christ by John Warr, by whose side Carey worked as a shoe cobbler. Charles Spurgeon was won by an uneducated "lay preacher." Add to this number millions of believers who were won by one. Simon Peter, won to Jesus by Andrew his brother, became the great preacher of Pentecost, when three thousand souls were saved (Acts 2:41). Have you found Jesus, the Bread of Life? Surely, then, there is someone with whom you can share the good news (John 3:16).

3. What others have said about Jesus. The early American patriot and unbeliever Thomas Paine said about Jesus, "The morality that He preached has not been exceeded by any." Thomas Jefferson, author of the Declaration of Independence, said: "Jesus Christ has given to us the most sublime and benevolent code of laws ever offered to man." Atheist Colonel Robert Ingersoll called Jesus only "a man among men." Lew

Wallace, author of *Ben Hur*, called Him "the Son of God." The Roman centurion at the cross said, "Truly this was the Son of God." And Judas Iscariot believed Jesus' worth was only thirty pieces of silver.

Before Jesus got personal with His question about His identity, He asked His disciples, "Whom do men say that I am?" (16:13–14). But the question was a personal question, and He pressed them for a personal answer. Peter responded for them all, "Thou art the Christ, the Son of the living God" (16:15–16).

What is your view of Jesus? Have you accepted Him as your Savior? You can if you will ask Him to come into your life right now and trust Him alone (Acts 16:31; Rom. 10:9–10).

4. The Great Confession. Peter confessed, "Thou art the Christ, the Son of the living God" (16:16). What Peter was saying from his heart was that he believed the man Jesus, whom he (Peter) had been following, was none other than the long-promised Messiah or Christ ("the Anointed One") promised by the prophets. What a magnificent leap of faith! Here was an uneducated fisherman, untrained in theology, who was convinced by the evidence he had seen. It is the same with us. Although we have not seen Him in the flesh, we who are His followers have been convinced by the evidence given in the Scriptures and witnessed to our hearts by the Holy Spirit, that Jesus is exactly who He claimed to be. Like Peter, not knowing all we would like to know, we received Him into our hearts as Savior and Lord by a childlike act of faith (Eph. 2:8–10).

5. The keys of the kingdom. Jesus told both Peter (v. 19) and the church (18:18) that the keys of the kingdom were given to them. Was he appointing Peter the pope of the church? No. He was placing in Peter's hands, and later into His church's hands, the keys—the gospel of salvation by grace through faith—that will open the gates to all who believe!

6. No other way. Two young boys were exploring when they came upon a cave in the side of the mountain. With their flashlights showing the way, they wandered deeply into the cave's interior. No light was visible from the outside, and they knew they must turn around and retrace their steps. By this time their flashlight had failed, and for hours they stumbled in the darkness trying to find the only way out. It was only when the boys heard the searchers calling their names that they were able to find the mouth of the cave and safety.

Jesus told His disciples that He must die and then be raised from the dead (16:21). Peter, not understanding the divine plan, rebuked Him (16:22). But Jesus told Peter that there was no other way for God to save a lost world (16:23). Jesus, alone, is the Light of the world.

TEACHING THE BIBLE

▶ *Main Idea:* We all must confess Jesus as the Messiah.

▶ *Suggested Teaching Aim:* To lead adults to confess Jesus as the Messiah.

A TEACHING OUTLINE

1. Use an illustration to begin the study.
2. Use a lesson outline poster and brief lectures to guide the Bible study.
4. Use discussion questions to apply the Scriptures.

Introduce the Bible Study

Use "What others have said about Jesus" from "Applying the Bible" to introduce the study. Say: Today's lesson examines what Peter said about Jesus.

Search for Biblical Truth

Point out the lesson on the unit poster used the past two weeks. Make and display the following lesson poster:

Peter	
Following Jesus	Matt. 4:18–20
Peter Confesses Jesus as the Christ	Matt. 16:13–16
Jesus Commends Peter	Matt. 16:17–19
Jesus Predicts His Death	Matt. 16:20–21
Jesus Rebukes Peter	Matt. 16:22–23

Either cover the points until you are ready to use them or write the headings on strips you can put up as you teach.

Uncover the first outline point ("Following Jesus"). Ask a volunteer to read Matthew 4:18–20. Use a map to locate the Sea of Galilee and the city of Capernaum (kuh PURR nay uhm) as possibly the place where this event occurred.

Lecture briefly covering the following points: (1) what "follow me" meant; (2) the meaning of "disciple;" (3) Jesus' previous contact with Peter; and (4) the meaning of "stone."

DISCUSS: If Jesus called you, what new name would He give you?

Uncover the second outline point ("Peter Confesses Jesus as the Christ"). Ask a volunteer to read 16:13–16. Locate Caesarea Philippi (about twenty-five miles north of the Sea of Galilee). Ask members to identify the names the disciples suggested people were calling Jesus. (John the Baptist, Elijah, Jeremiah, prophet.) Use "Studying the Bible" to explain why people suggested each of these titles.

DISCUSS: Based on the way you live, who do you say Jesus is? Do we really believe something if we do not act like it?

Uncover the third outline point ("Jesus Commends Peter"). Ask a volunteer to read 16:17–19. Using "Studying the Bible," lecture briefly, explaining: (1) the various meanings of the word "rock"; (2) the use of the word "church" in this context; (3) the meaning of "gates of hell"; and (4) the meaning of "keys of the kingdom." **IN ADVANCE,** enlist a member to read "Keys of the Kingdom," *Holman Bible Dictionary,* page 839, and prepare a two- to three-minute report to be presented at this time.

DISCUSS: What have you done with the keys to the kingdom God has given you?

Uncover the fourth outline point ("Jesus Predicts His Death"). Using "Studying the Bible," lecture briefly, explaining the following: (1) why Jesus warned His disciples not to tell who He was; (2) how Jesus taught His disciples the kind of Messiah He was.

DISCUSS: How do you try to make Christ into someone He is not?

Uncover the fifth outline point ("Jesus Rebukes Peter"). Using "Studying the Bible," lecture briefly, explaining the following: (1) what was Peter's idea of the Messiah; (2) Jesus' rebuke of Peter.

DISCUSS: How have your actions created a stumbling block for the cause of Christ?

Give the Truth a Personal Focus

Ask: Can you affirm beyond any shadow of doubt that Jesus is the Messiah of God? If so, what does that mean to you? Challenge members not to try to force Jesus to be something He is not just to fit their idea of who Jesus is.

Judas Iscariot

Basic Passages: Matthew 26:14–16, 20–25, 47–50; 27:1–5
Focal Passages: Matthew 26:14–16, 20–25, 47–50; 27:1–5

The name "Judas" is one of the hated names of human history. He is like Benedict Arnold and Quisling in that he practiced betrayal for a price. Only a friend or insider can commit betrayal. Whereas Arnold and Quisling betrayed their country, Judas betrayed Jesus the Savior.

▶ **Study Aim:** *To describe how Judas betrayed Jesus*

STUDYING THE BIBLE

OUTLINE AND SUMMARY

    I.   **Judas Bargained to Betray Jesus (Matt. 26:14–16)**
   II. **Jesus Predicted His Betrayal (Matt. 26:20–25)**
 III. **Judas Betrayed Jesus (Matt. 26:47–50)**
 IV. **Judas Reacted to Jesus' Condemnation (Matt. 27:1–5)**

Judas made a bargain with the enemies of Jesus to betray the Lord (26:14–16). At the Last Supper, Jesus let Judas know that He was aware of what Judas intended to do (26:20–25). Judas betrayed Jesus with a kiss (26:47–50). After Jesus was condemned by the Sanhedrin, Judas expressed remorse, returned the blood money, and hanged himself (27:1–5).

I. Judas Bargained to Betray Jesus (Matt. 26:14–16)

14 Then one of the twelve, called Judas Iscariot, went unto the chief priests,

15 And said unto them, What will ye give me, and I will deliver him unto you? And they covenanted with him for thirty pieces of silver.

16 And from that time he sought opportunity to betray him.

Two facts lie in the background of Judas's actions: (1) As Passover approached, Jesus told His disciples that the time was near when He would be betrayed and crucified (Matt. 26:1–2). (2) The high priest and other religious leaders were plotting to have Jesus killed (Matt. 26:3–5). Judas knew of Jesus' prediction because he had heard it. He probably suspected that the leaders were plotting to kill Jesus.

Judas took the initiative. The high priest and the other plotters did not seek out Judas; instead, he sought them out. They probably were surprised that one of Jesus' disciples would offer to betray Him, but they quickly accepted Judas's offer. They made a deal with him for thirty pieces of silver. From that time on, Judas was alert for an opportunity to betray Jesus.

Why did the plotters welcome a betrayer? Because Jesus was popular with many of the people, the religious leaders knew they might start a riot if they tried to seize Jesus when He was surrounded by friends (Matt. 26:5). Therefore, a betrayer offered a way for the enemies of Jesus to seize Him when few friends were with Him. A betrayer was also helpful because Judas knew the places where Jesus was most likely to be found.

Why did Judas offer to betray Jesus? The New Testament never gives a clear answer to that question. Several theories have been proposed. Most of the theories agree about two things: (1) Judas wanted Jesus to set up an earthly kingdom. (2) Judas had become convinced that Jesus was not going to set up such a kingdom, but was determined to lay down His life.

Building on those facts, one theory says that Judas betrayed Jesus hoping to force Jesus to use His power and thus bring in an earthly kingdom. Another theory is that when Judas became convinced that Jesus was determined to throw away His life, Judas decided to salvage for himself what he could. This latter theory stresses the selfishness in Judas's question, "What will ye give me, and I will deliver him unto you?"

The Bible text gives two clear indications of the horror of Judas's bargain: (1) The words "one of the twelve" remind the reader that Judas was one of Jesus' closest associates and presumably loyal friends. (2) The "thirty pieces of silver" would have reminded faithful Jews of the price of a slave (Exod. 21:32). Judas sold out the Savior for the price of a slave!

II. Jesus Predicted His Betrayal (Matt. 26:20–25)

20 Now when the even was come, he sat down with the twelve.

21 And as they did eat, he said, Verily I say unto you, that one of you shall betray me.

22 And they were exceeding sorrowful, and began every one of them to say unto him, Lord, Is it I?

Earlier Jesus had spoken of His betrayal (Matt. 26:1–2). At the Last Supper, Jesus revealed to the Twelve that one of them would be the betrayer. This announcement upset the disciples. Each asked if he was the betrayer. The wording of the question in verse 22 expects a "no" answer. It was as if each asked, "Lord, it's not I, is it?" None of the others thought himself capable of such a terrible act, but none knew for sure that he might not become the betrayer.

23 And he answered and said, He that dippeth his hand with me in the dish, the same shall betray me.

24 The Son of man goeth as it is written of him: but woe unto that man by whom the Son of man is betrayed! it had been good for that man if he had not been born.

25 Then Judas, which betrayed him, answered and said, Master, is it I? He said unto him, Thou hast said.

They were not sitting at a table as we do when we eat. They were reclining on cushions in the shape of a *U* with food placed in the middle. One dish contained a gravy into which each dipped his bread. Thus verse 23 merely reemphasized that one of those eating with Jesus would betray Him. Jesus said that He had come to lay down His life according to the Scriptures. But Jesus pronounced a severe judgment on the one who betrayed Him.

Then Judas asked the same question the others had asked. The only difference was that the others called Jesus "Lord," but Judas called Him "Master" or "Rabbi." Judas also worded his question as if to receive a negative answer, but Jesus told Judas that he was the betrayer. Jesus apparently did this in such a way that most of the others didn't realize what Jesus meant. John 13:21–27 shows that John was aware of what Jesus meant, but he apparently did not tell the others. Soon after Jesus revealed to Judas that He knew of his evil plans, Judas went out into the night (John 13:27).

If Jesus knew that Judas was going to betray Him, why didn't Jesus take steps to stop the betrayer? Jesus came to offer Himself voluntarily. None of those who acted in taking His life could have taken the Son of God if Jesus had not allowed them to do so. When He was arrested, one of the disciples prepared to defend Jesus with a sword. Jesus told him to put away the sword. Then He asked, "Thinkest thou not that I cannot now pray to the Father, and he shall presently give me twelve legions of angels?" (Matt. 26:53).

III. Judas Betrayed Jesus (Matt. 26:47–50)

47 And while he yet spake, lo, Judas, one of the twelve, came, and with him a great multitude with swords and staves, from the chief priests and elders of the people.

48 Now he that betrayed him gave them a sign, saying, Whomsoever I shall kiss, that same is he: hold him fast.

49 And forthwith he came to Jesus, and said, Hail, master; and kissed him.

50 And Jesus said unto him, Friend, wherefore art thou come? Then came they, and laid hands on Jesus, and took him.

After leaving the last supper, Judas acted to fulfill his part in the bargain to betray Jesus. The religious leaders sent with Judas a large group armed with swords and clubs. Most were temple police and Roman soldiers (John 18:12). Judas led this group to Gethsemane. He promised to give them a sign so they would know whom to arrest. In the darkness, some kind of sign was necessary.

Judas told them that he would greet Jesus with a kiss. This was a common greeting at that time. Pupils often greeted their teachers with a kiss, as a sign of respect and affection. When Judas spotted Jesus, he went up to him, said, "Greetings, teacher," and kissed Jesus. The word for "kissed" in verse 49 is the strong form of the verb. This shows that Judas made a strong outward show of affection as he betrayed Jesus.

Jesus called Judas "friend" or "comrade." Some Bible versions translate the words of Jesus in verse 50 as a statement rather than a question. In other words, Jesus may have told Judas to do what he had come for. If Jesus asked him "wherefore art thou come?" it was not because Jesus was unaware of why Judas came. Jesus had already told Judas that He knew what Judas planned to do. The question of verse 50, therefore, was not an inquiry, but a rebuke.

As in Matthew 26:14, verse 47 reminds the reader that Judas was "one of the twelve." Once again, these words underscore the horror of what Judas was doing. We are not surprised when our enemies seek to do us harm. We are shocked and hurt when our friends aid our enemies.

IV. Judas Reacted to Jesus' Condemnation (Matt. 27:1–5)

1 When the morning was come, all the chief priests and elders of the people took counsel against Jesus to put him to death:

2 And when they had bound him, they led him away, and delivered him to Pontius [PAHN tih uhs] Pilate [PIGH luht] the governor.

The Sanhedrin (san HEE druhn) had already tried and condemned Jesus in an illegal night trial (Matt. 26:57–68). They met early the next morning to ratify their action. They also met to send Jesus to the Roman procurator. The Jewish court had authority to decide religious issues, but they lacked the authority to condemn a prisoner to death (John 18:31). Since Pilate had that power, they brought Jesus to Pilate for sentencing.

3 Then Judas, which had betrayed him, when he saw that he was condemned, repented himself, and brought the thirty pieces of silver to the chief priests and elders,

4 Saying, I have sinned in that I have betrayed the innocent blood. And they said, What is that to us? see thou to it.

5 And he cast down the pieces of silver in the temple, and departed, and went and hanged himself.

After the Sanhedrin condemned Jesus and sent Him to Pilate for sentencing, Judas recognized the horror of what he had done. He had betrayed an innocent man, who was now on His way to die. Judas realized that the blood of the innocent Jesus would be on his hands.

Why did Judas have this sudden change of heart? As noted earlier, some Bible students believe that Judas betrayed Jesus in order to force Jesus to use His power and thus help set up an earthly kingdom. According to this theory, Judas was upset because he never expected Jesus actually to allow Himself to be executed. The other possibility is that Judas acted selfishly in betraying Jesus. In his mind, Judas knew he was betraying Jesus to those who intended to kill Him. However, when this was actually about to happen, Judas had a moment of truth. His conscience, which had been inactive, now awoke enough to show him the evil that he had done.

By contrast, the religious leaders seem to have totally suppressed their consciences. They shared none of Judas's second thoughts. When he came and told them that he had sinned by betraying innocent blood, the enemies of Jesus said in essence, "What do we care? Keep your regrets to yourself."

The word "repented" in verse 3 is not the usual word for true repentance, which involves sorrow for sin, turning from sin, and turning to God in trust. The word in verse 3 stresses the regret and remorse that Judas felt. Although Judas used the words "I have sinned," he was not expressing true repentance and faith. He lacked the trust to cast himself on God's mercy. Instead of confessing to God, he went to the callous Sanhedrin.

After Peter denied Jesus, he "went out, and wept bitterly" (Matt. 26:75). After the resurrection of Jesus, Peter was forgiven and restored to service. Judas responded to his sense of guilt and regret by hanging himself.

APPLYING THE BIBLE

1. The slow growth of evil. Roy Angell tells about a country preacher who came upon a farmer plowing between some rows of corn. "What are you doing?" asked the preacher. "I am plowing under the grass and weeds," said the farmer. "But the field is almost bare between the corn," the preacher replied. But the farmer had the last word. "Preacher, you know as well as I do that grass and weed seeds lie dormant here, and with the first spring rain these rows will be filled with grass and weeds unless I plow them under."

Evil grows slowly. Each of us has a sinful nature; and unless Jesus takes care of our sin problem, it will grow like a monstrous master within us.

So it was with Judas. When Jesus called Judas to follow Him, Jesus saw a lot of potential in Judas, though Jesus knew from the beginning that Judas would betray Him (John 6:64). The evil in Judas's heart grew slowly, just as it will in our hearts if it is not countered by the grace of God in Christ.

2. Selling out to sin. An artist in Italy once painted Mary and the Christ child. Years later, he was painting another New Testament scene, some say the Last Supper; and he needed someone to pose as Judas. Searching the prisons, he finally found his character; and day after day he went to the prison to sketch the man. But the more the artist visited the man, the more familiar he seemed. "Did I ever paint you?" the artist asked. "Yes," the man said shamefully. "My mother told me that when I was just a child, I posed for you as you painted Jesus on Mary's bosom."

So it was with Judas. He started well, but the race is not marked by how well one starts but how well one finishes! Judas sold out Jesus because Judas first sold out to sin. It is a warning to each of us. I have known too many Christians who started well only to finish tragically.

3. The bitter betrayal. Our lesson points out that the most infamous names in history are the betrayers, and Judas heads the list. But wait a minute! What about the person who hears the gospel again and again but refuses to yield his heart to the Savior? Has he not denied and betrayed the Savior who died for him? He knows that Jesus died for his sins, and that the Holy Spirit is convicting him. But to it all he gives a steadfast "No!" Does his or her sin not fall into the same category as Judas's sin? Vehemently, we would say it doesn't. But does it? Think about it. Jesus said it would have been good if Judas had not been born, for he will spend eternity in hell (26:24). But where will the rejector of Jesus spend eternity? The Bible gives the answer: with Judas in hell (Rev. 20:15; 21:8)!

4. The burning kiss. Can you remember the first kiss you received from a boyfriend or girlfriend? Do you remember your mother's kisses when you returned home from school? What about the first time you kissed your babies and the first time they put their wet lips on your cheeks?

Judas had told the chief priests he would give them a sign: "Seize the man I kiss and hold Him fast." According to Greek scholar A. T. Robertson, this means that he "kissed him fervently"! What hypocrisy! He who had laid His tender hands on the heads of little children and blessed them, is betrayed by a "fervent kiss!"

But mark it down: our affection for Jesus can be just as hypocritical! To be a friend of Jesus, He tells us, we must do as He commands us: "Ye are my friends, if ye do whatsoever I command you" (John 15:14). Are you a friend of Jesus?

5. Judas's remorse. A guilty conscience is a heavy burden to bear. John Randolph (1773–1833) was both a United States Representative and Senator. He had a cruel, biting tongue and opposed many popular measures that came before those bodies. When he used insulting language in opposing Henry Clay as Secretary of State, Clay challenged Randolph to a duel; but no blood was spilled. When he lay dying in Philadelphia, Randolph kept repeating, "Remorse! Remorse!" He asked for a dictionary so he could study the word, and when none could be found he had his physician write on a paper, "Remorse!"

There we have a picture of Judas overwhelmed, not by genuine repentance, but by remorse (27:3–5). He who made such a good start had a terrible and tragic end. What a poignant warning to each of us!

TEACHING THE BIBLE

▶ *Main Idea:* Each of us is capable of betraying Jesus.

▶ *Suggested Teaching Aim:* To lead adults to identify ways they are capable of betraying Jesus and to discover steps they can take to prevent it.

A TEACHING OUTLINE

1. Use an illustration to introduce the Bible study.

2. Use the unit poster and a lesson outline poster to show progression in the unit and the lesson.

3. Use Scripture search, questions and answers, and group discussion to search for biblical truth.

4. Use a poster to apply Bible study.

Introduce the Bible Study

Use "The slow growth of evil" from "Applying the Bible" to introduce the Bible study. Say: The lesson will examine how Judas betrayed Jesus.

Search for Biblical Truth

IN ADVANCE, write the following on large strips of paper and fasten them to the backs of four chairs:

1. Judas Bargained to Betray Jesus (Matt. 26:14–16)
2. Jesus Predicted His Betrayal (Matt. 26:20–25)
3. Judas Betrayed Jesus (Matt. 26:47–50)
4. Judas Reacted to Jesus' Condemnation (Matt. 27:1–5)

Point out today's lesson on the unit poster. Ask the person with the first outline point to place it on the focal wall. Ask members to read Matthew 26:14–16 silently. Point out that the Bible does not specifically tell us why Judas betrayed Jesus. Use "Studying the Bible" to explain possible motives Judas had for betraying Jesus.

DISCUSS: Why do you think Judas betrayed Jesus?

Ask the person with the second outline point to place it on the wall. Ask members to read silently Matthew 26:20–25. Using "Studying the Bible," explain (1) the eating custom involved in the supper; (2) Judas's use of "Master" instead of "Lord"; (3) why Jesus did not stop Judas.

DISCUSS: What warning signs of betrayal do you look for in your own behavior?

Ask the person who has the third outline point to place it on the focal wall. Ask members to read Matthew 26:47–50. Use a map to locate the garden of Gethsemane in relation to Jerusalem. Ask: Who came with Judas to arrest Jesus? (Jewish temple police and likely some mob elements.) What was the sign Judas had chosen to identify Jesus? (A kiss.) Why was a signal necessary? (It was dark, they had only torches for lights, and they were in a garden.) What did Jesus call Judas even after Judas had betrayed Him? (Friend.)

DISCUSS: How do you feel when an enemy hurts you? How do you feel when a friend betrays you? What makes the friend's betrayal so hurtful?

Ask the person with the fourth outline strip to place it on the wall. Ask members to read Matthew 27:1–5 silently. Ask: Why do you think Judas did what he did in these verses? What made him sorry for his actions? Was his repentance real? How did Judas's actions differ from Peter's?

DISCUSS: What do you think would have happened if Judas had waited around for the resurrection?

Give the Truth a Personal Focus

On a chalkboard or a large sheet of paper, write **Betrayal** in one column and **Prevention** in another. Ask members to suggest ways we betray Jesus today. List these on the chalkboard under **Betrayal.** Ask: Are our actions as bad as Judas's? What makes our actions different from Judas's? Are we ever safe from betraying Jesus?

Ask members to suggest steps they can take to keep themselves from betraying Jesus. List these under **Prevention.**

Remind members that the only betrayal Jesus cannot forgive is that which is not confessed. Stress that we are also just one action away from betrayal, but with the Holy Spirit's help we can refuse to betray our Lord.

Barnabas

Basic Passages: Acts 4:32–37; 9:23–31; 11:19–30
Focal Passages: Acts 4:32, 36–37; 9:26–27; 11:22–30

This lesson begins a four-lesson unit on "Persons of the New Testament Church." None of the early believers had a more attractive personality than Barnabas (BAHR nuh buhs). He is pictured in the New Testament as one who encouraged and helped others in the Christian way.

♦**Study Aim:** *To list examples of Barnabas as an encourager*

STUDYING THE BIBLE

OUTLINE AND SUMMARY

    I.   **Barnabas Gave Generously (Acts 4:32–37)**
        1. Oneness of the early church (4:32–35)
        2. Introduction of Barnabas (4:36–37)
   II. **Barnabas Welcomed Saul (Acts 9:23–31)**
  III. **Barnabas Encouraged the Antioch Church (Acts 11:19–30)**
        1. Helping a new church (11:19–24)
        2. Teaching new converts (11:25–26)
        3. Entrusted with a relief offering (11:27–30)

One expression of the oneness of the Jerusalem church was their sharing of possessions with those in need (4:32–35). Barnabas, son of encouragement, sold a field and gave the money to be shared with the needy (4:36–37). When the apostles feared Saul and didn't believe him, Barnabas encouraged Saul by sponsoring him for membership in the Jerusalem church. (9:23–31). Barnabas encouraged the new church at Antioch (AN tih ahk), which had taken a new direction by including Gentiles (11:19–24). Barnabas and Saul encouraged the Antioch church by spending a year teaching (11:25–26). Barnabas encouraged the Jerusalem church by joining Saul in taking an offering from the Antioch church (11:27–30).

I. Barnabas Gave Generously (Acts 4:32–37)

1. Oneness of the early church (4:32–35)

32 And the multitude of them that believed were of one heart and of one soul: neither said any of them that aught of the things which he possessed was his own; but they had all things common.

The Bible says that the early believers were a *koinonia* (Acts 2:42). English translations often use the word "fellowship" to describe what *koinonia* means, but the word means more than what we usually mean by "fellowship." *Koinonia* refers to the common life that believers share because of their relationship with God through Jesus Christ (1 John 1:3).

One expression of this oneness in the Jerusalem church was the sharing of material possessions. This is mentioned in Acts 2:44–45 and 4:32–37. Because they were of one heart and one soul, they voluntarily shared with one another. They continued to reach out to nonbelievers as the apostles bore witness to the resurrection of the Lord Jesus (v. 33). They cared for one another as those that had possessions sold them and brought the money for distribution to the needy (vv. 34–35).

2. Introduction of Barnabas (4:36–37)

36 And Joses (JOH seez), who by the apostles was surnamed Barnabas, (which is, being interpreted, The son of consolation,) a Levite, and of the country of Cyprus,

37 Having land, sold it, and brought the money, and laid it at the apostles' feet.

Acts 4:36–37 introduces a personality of the early church who played a major role in later events. These verses tell about a man named Joseph (or Joses). He was originally from Cyprus, but was now living in Jerusalem. He was a Levite, a group originally set aside for temple service. Although Levites originally owned no land (Deut. 10:9; Num. 18:20, 24), this seems no longer to have been true; because Joseph was a land owner.

Joseph was an outstanding example of the practice described in verses 32–35. Joseph sold his land, brought the money, and laid it at the apostles' feet for distribution to needy members of the church. This action and his later actions led the apostles to give Joseph a nickname. They called him Barnabas, which means "son of encouragement." The word translated "consolation" has a broader meaning than what we usually mean by "consolation." Barnabas did more than console people in sorrow; he encouraged them in a variety of situations.

II. Barnabas Welcomed Saul (Acts 9:23–31)

After Saul's conversion, he continued as a bold witness in Damascus (duh MASS cuss; Acts 9:20–22). His preaching was so effective that his enemies plotted to kill him (v. 23). When Saul and his friends discovered that enemies were watching the gates day and night (v. 24), they lowered Saul over the wall of the city in a basket (v. 25).

26 And when Saul was come to Jerusalem, he assayed to join himself to the disciples: but they were all afraid of him, and believed not that he was a disciple.

27 But Barnabas took him, and brought him to the apostles, and declared unto them how he had seen the Lord in the way, and that he had spoken to him, and how he had preached boldly at Damascus in the name of Jesus.

The last time Saul was in Jerusalem, he was a relentless persecutor of believers in Jesus (Acts 8:1–3). He had gone to Damascus to continue his angry persecution (Acts 9:1–2). Therefore, when Saul returned to Jerusalem, the apostles' memories of him caused them to fear him. The apostles had probably heard what Saul was saying about his encounter with the Lord and of the Lord's commission to him (Acts 9:3–16). However, the apostles didn't believe Saul. They no doubt suspected that he was laying an elaborate trap to ensnare followers of Jesus.

At this point, Barnabas intervened on behalf of Saul. He brought Saul to the apostles. Barnabas then told them how the Lord had appeared to Saul and had spoken to him. Barnabas also told the apostles of Saul's bold testimony for Christ in Damascus. By doing this, Barnabas risked his reputation and perhaps his life as well. He had no way of knowing for sure that Saul was a true convert, but Barnabas was willing to take the risk. He stood up for Saul when no one else did.

As a result, Saul was accepted and began sharing church fellowship (v. 28) and bearing testimony for Christ in Jerusalem. Saul's preaching was so effective that his enemies were determined to kill him (v. 29). As a result, the brothers in Christ took Saul to Caesarea, where he sailed back to his native Tarsus (TAHR sus; v. 30). As a result of the conversion of this former persecutor and his bold preaching, churches throughout the entire region were strengthened (v. 31). Saul of Tarsus later became Paul the great missionary. His name overshadows the name of Barnabas in the Bible, but consider the key role that Barnabas played in Saul's life. He sponsored Saul at a crucial stage in the life of this new convert with so much promise.

III. Barnabas Encouraged the Antioch Church (Acts 11:19–30)

1. Helping a new church (11:19–24)

After the death of Stephen, believers were scattered from Jerusalem; and wherever they went, they preached the good news (Acts 8:4). Some of the believers went to the city of Antioch and preached Jesus to their fellow Jews (v. 19). Some of the Jewish believers, however, began to preach to Greeks (v. 20). Because God was with them in such bold witness, many believed and turned to the Lord (v. 21).

22 Then tidings of these things came unto the ears of the church which was in Jerusalem: and they sent forth Barnabas, that he should go as far as Antioch.

23 Who, when he came, and had seen the grace of God, was glad, and exhorted them all, that with purpose of heart they would cleave unto the Lord.

24 For he was a good man and full of the Holy Ghost and of faith: and much people was added unto the Lord.

Including Gentiles as well as Jews in the church was something new. It is true that Peter had been to Cornelius, but little had been done to follow up by the Jerusalem believers (Acts 10:1–11:18). The Jerusalem church expressed an interest in the new direction by sending Barnabas to see what was going on in Antioch. Barnabas was a good choice for such a delicate mission. He was a good man who was led by God's Spirit.

Barnabas saw what was happening in Antioch as evidence of God's grace at work. Rather than rebuking them for their inclusion of Gentiles in the church, Barnabas encouraged the Antioch believers to remain true to the Lord with all their hearts. As a result of such encouragement, the Lord was able to continue to add new converts to their number.

2. Teaching new converts (11:25–26)

25 Then departed Barnabas to Tarsus, for to seek Saul:

26 And when he had found him, he brought him unto Antioch. And it came to pass, that a whole year they assembled themselves with the church, and taught much people. And the disciples were called Christians first in Antioch.

Barnabas realized that the new converts needed to be taught. He decided to go and get Saul to help him. Thus Barnabas went to Tarsus and found Saul. Then they returned to Antioch and spent an entire year with the church. During that year these two choice leaders taught many people. Thus Barnabas the encourager helped both Saul and the believers at Antioch. Earlier, Barnabas had stood up for Saul when he wanted to join the Jerusalem church. Now Barnabas helped Saul by enlisting him in work that eventually launched Saul as a missionary (Acts 13:1–4). Barnabas continued his encouraging role as he and Saul taught the church.

The Antioch disciples were the first to be called Christians. They had been called disciples, brothers, or believers. The name "Christian" appears only two other times in the New Testament (Acts 26:28; 1 Pet. 4:16). Each reference suggests that the name was first used by nonbelievers to describe followers of Christ. The title means those belonging to or having been identified with Christ, and it may originally have been intended as a term of derision.

3. Entrusted with a relief offering (11:27–30)

27 And in these days came prophets from Jerusalem unto Antioch.

28 And there stood up one of them named Agabus [AG uh buhs], and signified by the spirit that there should be great dearth throughout all the world: which came to pass in the days of Claudius [KLAW dih uhs] Caesar [SEE zur].

29 Then the disciples, every man according to his ability, determined to send relief unto the brethren which dwelt in Judaea:

30 Which also they did, and sent it to the elders by the hands of Barnabas and Saul.

Among a group of prophets who came from Jerusalem was a prophet named Agabus. The same man appeared later to speak a prophecy concerning Paul (Acts 21:10–11). Agabus had the gift to foresee some future events. He told the Antioch church that a severe and widespread famine was coming. Luke adds that such a famine actually came during the reign of Claudius Caesar (A.D. 41–54).

The Antioch church responded to this prediction by deciding to send financial help to their brothers in Judea. We are not told why they concentrated on Judea. Perhaps Agabus indicated that the famine would be especially hard there. Perhaps since many of the Antioch believers had come from Jerusalem, they knew the large number of poor in the church and the growing hostility of unbelievers. Perhaps the Antioch church wanted to show their Jewish brothers that a Jew-Gentile church could demonstrate Christian love. Paul later asked for an offering from Gentile churches for these reasons (Rom. 15:25–27; 2 Cor. 8–9).

At any rate, the Antioch church followed the principle of voluntary giving according to one's ability. Then they asked Barnabas and Saul to carry the offering to Jerusalem. This shows how much the Antioch church trusted and respected these two choice leaders. Earlier, Barnabas had helped needy disciples in Jerusalem by giving his own money. Now he and Saul helped and encouraged the Jerusalem church with this love offering from their brothers and sisters in Antioch.

APPLYING THE BIBLE

1. William McKinley's philosophy. When William McKinley, the twenty-fifth president of the United States, was elected governor of Ohio, he considered appointing a bitter opponent to a high office in the state. When McKinley was challenged by one of his advisors, McKinley replied he felt the man was the best qualified for the job. Then, he added with a smile: "If we spend all our time getting even, we shall never get ahead."

The church at Jerusalem had its problems which later emerged; but at the outset it was interested in getting ahead, so the people had to be united and pull together (Acts 4:32–35). And the church did get ahead. According to New Testament scholar Henry Clarence Thiessen, by A.D. 65 the Jerusalem church may have had as many as twenty thousand members.[1] Any church that wants to get ahead and stay ahead must pull together. It's called *unity.*

2. A sacrificial church. A plaque in the Alamo reads: "It was here that a gallant few, the bravest of the brave, threw themselves between the enemy and the settlements, determined never to surrender nor retreat. They redeemed their pledge to Texas with the forfeit of their lives. They fell the chosen sacrifice to Texas freedom."

The Jerusalem church was a sacrificing church (4:32–35). They shared what they had—their lives, their all—with each other to protect the needy in their fellowship. Those able to do so "threw themselves between the enemy"—hunger and privation—and the less fortunate.

With the needs of our world so great, we ought to move out of our stingy giving to follow the example of "the mother church."

3. Barnabas leads the way. The New International Version translates the name of Barnabas as "Son of Encouragement" (4:36). He was devout and wealthy. Also, he was unselfish (4:37). Seeking no applause for himself, he sold his land, brought the proceeds, and laid them at the apostles' feet. What a marvelous and unselfish example he set! The church took note of it, and he is memorialized in Scripture for his generosity.

I grew up in Oklahoma, often hearing my father tell this story. He was helping take the offering one Sunday morning in our church. It was during the years of the Great Depression and the church was struggling financially. When he passed the plate to a certain doctor that morning, the doctor laid a folded bill in the plate, covering it with his hand as though he did not want his gift to be seen. When, later, the morning offering was counted, the bill was unfolded and found, to the shock of the money-counter, to be a $1,000 bill. My father treasured the story and appreciated the doctor for his sacrificial gift that made so much difference to a struggling church.

That's the Barnabas spirit!

4. "Mr. Encourager." We can call Barnabas "Mr. Encourager." Everywhere we see him in the Scriptures, Barnabas has his arm around someone saying, "You can make it" (Acts 9:26–27; 11:19–24; 25–26; 27–30)! And don't forget John Mark (15:36–41). Had it not been for Barnabas, Saul (Paul) would not have been received by the church (9:26–29). If it had not been for Barnabas, Paul might have stayed in Tarsus and been lost to the great missionary enterprise to the Gentiles (11:25–26). It is to Paul's discredit that he wanted to write young Mark off (15:36–39). But it is to Barnabas's credit that he took Mark in. Had it not been for Barnabas, we would not have the Gospel of Mark. What a Christian was Barnabas!

5. The thing everybody needs. Everybody needs encouragement! Young Fanny was blinded in 1826 when she was only six weeks old. But her grandmother became Fanny's eyes, telling her about the beauties of nature. When Fanny showed an interest in poetry, her grandmother encouraged her. The next time you sing Fanny Crosby's "Blessed Assurance, Jesus Is Mine" or "Jesus Keep Me Near the Cross," give thanks for a grandmother who encouraged a little blind girl.

Remember: Few need your criticism, but everybody needs your encouragement!

TEACHING THE BIBLE

▶ *Main Idea:* Encouraging others is a mark of a mature Christian.

▶ *Suggested Teaching Aim:* To lead members to identify how they can become encouragers.

A TEACHING OUTLINE

1. *Use an illustration to introduce the lesson.*

2. *Use member-created questions to examine the Bible.*

3. *Use listing to apply the Bible.*

Introduce the Bible Study

Prepare the following unit poster.

Persons of the New Testament Church		
Barnabas	Acts 4:32–37; 9:23–31; 11:19–30	February 2
Stephen	Acts 6:1–8:3	February 9
Priscilla and Aquila	Acts 18:1–4, 18–19, 24–26; Rom. 16:3–5a	February 16
Timothy	Acts 16:1–5; 1 Cor. 4:14–17; Phil. 2:19–24; 2 Tim. 1:3–7; 3:14–15	February 23

Use "Barnabas leads the way" in "Applying the Bible" to introduce the lesson. Locate the lesson on the unit poster.

Search for Biblical Truth

IN ADVANCE, write each of the following on a strip of paper. Fasten each strip to the wall as you teach.

Barnabas Encouraged Others by . . .	
1. Giving Generously	Acts 4:32,36–37
2. Supporting Saul	Acts 9:26–27
3. Helping a New Church	Acts 11:22–24
4. Teaching New Converts	Acts 11:25–26
5. Collecting an Offering	Acts 11:27–30

Place strips around the room at random. As you come to each point, place the proper strip on the focal wall.

Place the first strip on the focal wall. Tell members that you are going to play "Ask the Teacher." Ask members to read silently Acts 4:32, 36–37 and to compose one question each based on this passage to ask you. Be sure the following information is shared either in the form of answers or in a brief lecture (or use these for questions to ask members if they cannot come up with questions for you): (1) What is the meaning of the word *koinonia?* (2) Why did the believers in Jerusalem share with the needy? (3) What was Barnabas's tribal and national background? (4) What was Barnabas's act of generosity? (5) What was Barnabas's nickname?

Place the second strip on the focal wall. Ask members to read silently Acts 9:26–27 and to compose one question each based on this passage to ask you. Be sure the following information is shared: (1) What had happened to Saul since he had left Jerusalem? (2) Why were the Jerusalem disciples afraid of Saul? (3) How did Barnabas befriend Saul? (4) How would you have responded if you had been in Jerusalem?

Place the third strip on the focal wall. Ask members to read silently Acts 11:22–24 and to compose one question each based on this passage to ask you. Be sure the following information is shared: (1) Why was Barnabas sent to Antioch? (2) What was Barnabas's response to the situation in Antioch? (3) Why was Antioch so significant?

Place the fourth strip on the wall. Ask members to read silently Acts 11:25–26 and to compose one question each based on this passage to ask you. Be sure the following facts are shared: (1) Why do you think Barnabas went after Saul? (2) What did they do in Antioch to help the church?

Place the fifth strip on the focal wall. Ask members to read silently Acts 11:27–30 and to compose one question each based on this passage to ask you. Be sure the following information is shared: (1) Who prophesied that a famine was coming? (2) Why do you think the disciples chose Barnabas as one of the bearers of the offering to Jerusalem?

Give the Truth a Personal Focus

Review how Barnabas encouraged. Ask members to suggest ways they can be encouragers. List these on a chalkboard or a large sheet of paper. Ask them to choose at least one specific way they could be an encourager this week.

---

1. Henry Clarence Thiessen, *Introducing the New Testament* (Grand Rapids, Mich.: William B. Eerdmans Publishing Co., 1951), 136.

Stephen

Basic Passage: Acts 6:1–8:3
Focal Passages: Acts 6:8–15; 7:54–60

Stephen is first mentioned as one of the seven chosen to serve tables, but he quickly became one of the boldest spokesmen for Christ. His testimony was so effective that the enemies of Christ put Stephen to death. The way he lived and the way he died are examples for later generations of believers.

♦**Study Aim:** *To show how Stephen was a bold witness for Christ by how he lived and how he died*

STUDYING THE BIBLE

OUTLINE AND SUMMARY

    I. **Selection of the Seven (Acts 6:1–7)**
   II. **Reaction to Stephen's Words and Deeds (Acts 6:8–15)**
       1. Power of Stephen's words and deeds (6:8–10)
       2. A campaign of lies (6:11–15)
  III. **Stephen's Speech to the Sanhedrin (Acts 7:1–53)**
       1. The patriarchs (7:1–16)
       2. Moses (7:17–34)
       3. History of rebellion (7:35–53)
  IV. **Stephen's Death (Acts 7:54–8:3)**
       1. Stephen's response to the mob's fury (7:54–56)
       2. Stephen's dying prayers (7:57–60)
       3. Aftermath (8:1–3)

Stephen was one of the seven chosen to oversee the distribution of food to widows (6:1–7). His words and deeds aroused opposition among Greek-speaking Jews (6:8–10). They mounted a campaign of lies that aroused the people and Sanhedrin (san HEE drun; 6:11–15). Stephen spoke to the Sanhedrin about Abraham, who never owned land in Canaan, and Joseph, who delivered his people by bringing them to Egypt (7:1–16). Moses was raised as an Egyptian, was rejected by his people, and received God's revelation at Mount Sinai (SIGH nay igh; 7:17–34). The Israelites had rebelled against God, rejected the prophets, and killed the Messiah (7:35–53). When the mob expressed its fury, Stephen spoke of seeing the Son of Man in heaven (7:54–56). As Stephen was stoned, he committed himself to the Lord and prayed for his executioners (7:57–60). As devout people buried Stephen, Saul launched a violent persecution of those who shared Stephen's faith (8:1–3).

I. Selection of the Seven (Acts 6:1–7)

The Greek-speaking widows in the Jerusalem church complained that they were being neglected in the daily distribution of food (v. 1). When the Twelve proposed that the church select seven men to oversee the distribution, Stephen was one of those selected (vv. 2–6). As a result, the word of God spread and the church grew (v. 7).

II. Reaction to Stephen's Words and Deeds (Acts 6:8–15)

1. Power of Stephen's words and deeds (6:8–10)

8 And Stephen, full of faith and power, did great wonders and miracles among the people.

9 Then there arose certain of the synagogue, which is called the synagogue of the Libertines [LIB ur teens], and Cyrenians [sigh REE nih uhns], and Alexandrians [al eg ZAN drih uhns], of them of Cilicia [sih LISH ih uh] and of Asia, disputing with Stephen.

10 And they were not able to resist the wisdom and the spirit by which he spake.

One of the qualifications for the seven was that they be "of honest report, full of the Holy Ghost and wisdom" (Acts 6:3). In the biblical list of the seven, Stephen's name is listed first; and he is described as "a man full of faith and of the Holy Ghost" (Acts 6:5). Stephen was selected because the church saw these qualities in him. Their choice was confirmed by what Stephen did after he was chosen. Stephen's actions clearly showed that he was "full of faith and power."

Stephen was not content to confine his service to overseeing the distribution of food to widows. He was the first person other than the apostles to be described as working miracles. Verse 10 shows that Stephen also spoke the word of God with effectiveness.

Such effective service soon aroused opposition. The groups named in verse 9 represent Jews who had lived outside the holy land. "Libertines" in this verse means "freedmen," apparently a synagogue of ex-slaves; but the other names are places outside Judea: Cyrene, Alexandria, Cilicia, and Asia (the Roman province, not the continent). Since Stephen's name was Greek, he too was probably one of the many Jews who had lived away from Judea. Thus the opposition to Stephen arose among the group from which he had come. They saw him as a traitor to them and their ways. They argued with Stephen, but his words showed such wisdom and spirit that his opponents lost the debate.

2. A campaign of lies (6:11–15)

11 Then they suborned men, which said, We have heard him speak blasphemous words against Moses, and against God.

12 And they stirred up the people, and the elders, and the scribes, and came upon him, and caught him, and brought him to the council,

After being unable to defeat Stephen in debate, his enemies resorted to a campaign of lies. They persuaded a number of men to participate in telling these lies throughout Jerusalem. The gist of the lies was that Stephen was guilty of blasphemy because he was speaking against Moses and God.

They were so successful at spreading these lies that they were able to stir up two crucial groups. For the first time in Acts, the people of the city were aroused against the cause of Christ. Prior to this time, the people had been favorably disposed or at least neutral (Acts 2:47; 3:11; 4:21; 5:26). Now they were aroused against Stephen by the campaign of lies.

The other group was the Jewish council or Sanhedrin, which consisted of the elders and the scribes. This was the group that had set out to kill Jesus. They had been divided about how to deal with the work of the apostles (Acts 5:33–40), but now they were aroused by the lies. Stephen's enemies acted quickly. They seized him and took him to the Sanhedrin.

13 And set up false witnesses, which said, This man ceaseth not to speak blasphemous words against this holy place, and the law:

14 For we have heard him say, that this Jesus of Nazareth shall destroy this place, and shall change the customs which Moses delivered us.

The campaign of lies continued during Stephen's hearing before the Sanhedrin. The witnesses claimed to have heard Stephen say that Jesus of Nazareth would destroy the holy temple and would change the traditions given by Moses. The two groups in the Sanhedrin were the priestly party or Sadducees (SAD joo sees) and the legal party or Pharisees (FER uh sees; see Matt. 15:1–9). The Sadducees were concerned about maintaining their control over the temple. The Pharisees were concerned about preserving their interpretations of the Mosaic law. The enemies of Stephen cleverly included both charges in order to mobilize both Sadducees and Pharisees against Stephen.

Throughout the account of Stephen's trial and death are numerous parallels to Jesus' trial and death. During the trial of Jesus, false witnesses claimed that He said He would destroy the temple (Matt. 26:60–61; Mark 14:57–58). A similar charge was made against Stephen. During His life, Jesus was often accused of departing from the Mosaic customs. What He departed from were the human traditions that had grown up and become sanctified by the Pharisees.

15 And all that sat in the council, looking stedfastly on him, saw his face as it had been the face of an angel.

During the trial, Stephen's face shone like that of an angel. Rather than faltering before this barrage of lies, Stephen shone with the light of truth. God gave this as a sign of His favor.

III. Stephen's Speech to the Sanhedrin (Acts 7:1–53)

1. The patriarchs (7:1–16)

Stephen's speech was a carefully crafted response to the false charges against him. Two themes run through the speech: (1) God has never been bound to one place. (2) Israel has repeatedly rejected the word of God. Abraham, for example, was a pilgrim of faith who never actually owned land in Canaan (vv. 1–8). Joseph, who was sold by the other patriarchs, became their deliverer, which involved moving to Egypt (vv. 9–16).

2. Moses (7:17–34)

Moses was raised as an Egyptian (vv. 17–22). When he tried to help the Hebrews, they rejected him (vv. 23–29). God revealed Himself to Moses at Mount Sinai (vv. 30–34).

3. History of rebellion (7:35–53)

The Israelites rebelled repeatedly in the wilderness (vv. 35–43). When Solomon built the temple, he acknowledged that God rules over the universe and does not dwell in one building (vv. 44–50). Directly addressing his accusers, Stephen accused them of killing the Messiah (vv. 51–53).

IV. Stephen's Death (Acts 7:54–8:3)

1. Stephen's response to the mob's fury (7:54–56)

54 When they heard these things, they were cut to the heart, and they gnashed on him with their teeth.

55 But he, being full of the Holy Ghost, looked up stedfastly into heaven, and saw the glory of God, and Jesus standing on the right hand of God,

56 And said, Behold, I see the heavens opened, and the Son of man standing on the right hand of God.

Those who had been listening to Stephen became infuriated at what he said. They were so angry that they gnashed their teeth. By contrast, Stephen was filled with the Spirit and saw a heavenly vision, which he described. During His ministry, Jesus repeatedly referred to Himself as the Son of man. Stephen's use of this title shows his understanding of Jesus' purpose and mission. God rewarded Stephen's faithfulness by opening heaven and allowing Stephen to see the Son of man. Stephen bore testimony to Christ by telling his enemies what he saw.

2. Stephen's dying prayers (7:57–60)

57 Then they cried out with a loud voice, and stopped their ears, and ran upon him with one accord,

58 And cast him out of the city, and stoned him: and the witnesses laid down their clothes at a young man's feet, whose name was Saul.

59 And they stoned Stephen, calling upon God, and saying, Lord Jesus, receive my spirit.

60 And he kneeled down, and cried with a loud voice, Lord, lay not this sin to their charge. And when he had said this, he fell asleep.

Because they had believed the lies about Stephen, most of his hearers had made up their minds about him much earlier. His speech only infuriated them, and his words about the Son of man in heaven were all they could stand. They stopped up their ears as a sign that Stephen was speaking blasphemy, rushed him out of the city, and proceeded to stone him. Luke mentioned in passing that those who stoned Stephen laid their clothes at the feet of Saul, who would become prominent later in the Book of Acts.

As Stephen was dying, he prayed two prayers that are similar to two of Jesus' prayers from the cross. As Jesus was being crucified, He prayed, "Father, forgive them; for they know not what they do" (Luke 23:34). As He died, He prayed, "Father, into thy hands I commend my spirit" (Luke 23:46). Stephen was the first Christian martyr. His dying, like his living, was a faithful reflection of the Lord in whom he believed and whom he served. What more can any believer hope for than to be as faithful in how we live and how we die (see Phil. 1:20)!

3. Aftermath (8:1–3)

Stephen's death was a watershed for the Christian movement. Stephen's life and death set the stage for the expansion of the gospel to all kinds of people. Saul's immediate reaction was to launch a persecution of all who shared Stephen's views (v. 1). As devout people mourned and buried Stephen, Saul launched a violent persecution (vv. 2–3).

APPLYING THE BIBLE

1. The "crowned one." Stephen's name means "crown," and what a marvelous spiritual crown he wore! Read the verses again in today's lesson and marvel at his spiritual character. This is the kind of people we need in our churches today: pious, godly, filled with the Holy Spirit, soul-winners, sacrificial. These qualities shine brightly against the backdrop of how many Christians behave themselves today—in church and out of church.

On his deathbed, Horace Greeley (1812–1872), founder and editor of *The New York Tribune,* said, "Fame is a vapor, popularity an accident, riches take wings; those who cheer today will curse tomorrow; only one thing endures—character."

Today, God give us Christian men and women of character like Stephen who will not blindly follow the masses.

2. The witnessing laymen. Stephen was not one of the Twelve officially called and set apart to preach, but preach he did (6:10; 7:1–53). And it resulted in his death (7:54–60).

Later, baptism and the Lord's Supper developed into "magical" rites with saving grace in them. This pagan idea demanded that these "magic" rites could only be preserved and administered by those who were trained and qualified to administer them. Thus the chasm developed between what today are called "the clergy" and the "the laity." "Clergy" means "those who have been called of God" and "laity" means "the people."[1] Certainly, God calls some to the sacred task of pastoring and preaching; but all, like Stephen, are to be evangelists—"good news tellers."

Our laity today find a good example in Brother Stephen.

3. The terrible power of a lie. Henry Ward Beecher said, "Even a liar tells a hundred truths to one lie; he has to, to make a lie good for anything." Even those from whose group Stephen had come (6:8–10) lied about what Stephen had said and done because they were unable "to resist the wisdom and the spirit by which he spoke" (v. 10). Like Jesus, his Lord, it appears that Stephen was sold out by his friends!

The lie spread like wildfire, as lies always do (vv. 11–14). More liars joined in and when Stephen was brought before the religious officials, he was condemned to death, not on the basis of truth, but of lies (vv. 13–14; 7:54–83).

Once a lie is out, it cannot be recalled. In spite of the liar's best efforts, it spreads like a raging fire (see James 3:1–12). A woman had been guilty of lying about her neighbor. Smitten by her conscience, she sought the counsel of her pastor. "Take a feather pillow," the pastor said, "shake out all the feathers, then go and gather each up and put it back in the pillow." "But that is impossible," the woman explained! "Exactly," said the pastor. "Your lies can never be recalled. They will go on and on hurting the neighbor against whom you spoke."

We ought to be very careful what we say about someone else. Even if we know it is true, we are under no obligation to pass it on.

4. The face of an angel. Devotional writer Virginia Ely tells of two brothers who were convicted of stealing sheep. As was the custom for sheep thieves in their country, the brothers were branded with the letters, "ST"—"sheep thief"—on their foreheads. One of the brothers was so ashamed that he moved to a far country and finally died in despair. The other stayed at home, lived an exemplary life, regained his character, and lived to be an old man. Many years later, a stranger to the area asked one who lived there the meaning of the letters. "I really don't know," the native replied, "it happened so many years ago. But I think it stands for saint!"

Stephen was branded and tried as a liar. But as he stood before the council "all that sat in the council . . . saw his face as it had been the face of an angel" (v. 15).

5. Stephen's homecoming welcome. After Christ's sufferings and resurrection, He ascended to heaven and sat down at the Father's right hand (Heb. 1:3). But Stephen, being stoned to death, saw Jesus "standing on the right hand of God" (7:56). Here is Jesus, pictured as arising from His throne, to welcome the first martyr home to glory! What a magnificent picture it is!

TEACHING THE BIBLE

▶ *Main Idea:* Christ calls us to be bold witnesses for Him.

▶ *Suggested Teaching Aim:* To lead adults to identify ways they can become bold witnesses for Christ.

A TEACHING OUTLINE

1. Use an illustration to introduce the lesson.

2. Use a chart to compare similarities between Stephen's and Jesus' death.

3. Use group discussion to search for biblical truth.

4. Use a thought question and brainstorming to give the truth a personal focus.

Introduce the Bible Study

Use "The witnessing layman" to introduce the lesson. Remind members that Stephen—a layman—was the first Christian martyr.

Search for Biblical Truth

Point out the lesson on the unit poster you made for February 2. On a chalkboard or a large sheet of paper write: **Similarities Between Jesus' and Stephen's Lives**. As you move through the lesson, list similarities as members mention them. (Some suggestions are made, but use members' ideas when possible.)

Read aloud Acts 6:8–10. Ask: Who was Stephen? To what office was he elected? How does the Bible describe him? What ministries did he perform? (*Chart*: Performed wonders and miracles.)

DISCUSS: Why do some people reject freedom and feel the need to control those who differ with them?

Read aloud 6:11–15. Ask: How did Stephen's enemies respond to his teaching? What lie did they tell? Who testified against him at his trial? With what crime was Stephen charged? (*Chart*: Arrested by a mob; testified against by false witnesses; charged with blasphemy.)

DISCUSS: What do you do when someone lies about you?

Summarize briefly the material in "III. Stephen's Speech to the Sanhedrin" in "Studying the Bible" to help members to understand the charges against Stephen and Stephen's defense.

Read aloud 7:54–8:3. Ask: Why do you think the council of the Sanhedrin reacted as they did to Stephen's defense? How did Stephen respond to their anger? How do you think this made his enemies feel? What was Stephen's response as he was being stoned? (*Chart*: Responded nonviolently; prayed as he died; forgave enemies.)

DISCUSS: What effect did Stephen's "turning the other cheek" have on his enemies? Is turning the other cheek always the best policy? Why doesn't turning the other cheek provide physical blessing for the person? Do you need to forgive someone who has wounded you?

Give the Truth a Personal Focus

Ask: If you had been present at Stephen's trial and stoning, which character would you have been: Stephen? his persecutor? uninterested bystander? part of the mob? Paul? those who buried Stephen? Ask members to respond.

Read the Teaching Aim: "To lead adults to identify ways they can become bold witnesses for Christ." Ask: What do you think enabled Stephen to bear such a bold witness for Christ? What steps can you take to become a bold witness for Christ? List members' suggestions on a chalkboard or a large sheet of paper. Ask members to choose those steps that would apply to their lives. Distribute paper and pencils and let them write how they will put these steps into practice. Let them keep the paper. Close in a time of commitment and prayer.

---

1. Robert A. Baker, *A Summary of Christian History*, revised by John M. Landers (Nashville: Broadman & Holman, 1994), 38.

Priscilla and Aquila

Basic Passages: Acts 18:1–4,18–19, 24–26; Romans 16:3–5a
Focal Passages: Acts 18:1–4,18–19, 24–26; Romans 16:3–5a

Priscilla (prih SIL uh) and Aquila (uh KWIL uh) are always mentioned together. They showed their commitment in several ways: sharing their home and work with Paul, instructing Apollos (uh PAHL uhs), risking their lives for Paul, providing a meeting place for the church, and faithfully serving Christ wherever they moved.

▶**Study Aim:** *To identify ways Priscilla and Aquila showed commitment to Christ*

STUDYING THE BIBLE

OUTLINE AND SUMMARY
  I. In Corinth (Acts 18:1–4)
  II. In Ephesus (Acts 18:18–19, 24–26)
     1. From Corinth to Ephesus (18:18–19)
     2. Helping Apollos (18:24–26)
  III. In Rome (Rom. 16:3–5a)

Priscilla and Aquila shared their home and work with Paul while he was in Corinth (KAWR inth; Acts 18:1–4). When Paul left Corinth, they moved to Ephesus (EF uh suhs; Acts 18:18–19). When Apollos came to Ephesus, they instructed him more completely in the Christian way (Acts 18:24–26). When Paul wrote to Rome, he greeted Priscilla and Aquila as helpers, thanked God that they had risked their lives for him, and greeted the church meeting in their house (Rom. 16:3–5a).

I. In Corinth (Acts 18:1–4)

1 After these things Paul departed from Athens, and came to Corinth;

2 And found a certain Jew named Aquila, born in Pontus [PAHN tuhs], lately come from Italy, with his wife Priscilla; (because that Claudius had commanded all Jews to depart from Rome:) and came unto them.

3 And because he was of the same craft, he abode with them, and wrought: for by their occupation they were tentmakers.

4 And he reasoned in the synagogue every sabbath, and persuaded the Jews and the Greeks.

Priscilla and Aquila are first mentioned during Paul's first visit to Corinth. This happened during Paul's second missionary journey. He came to Corinth from Athens (Acts 17:15–34). Corinth was a seaport town in Greece, the Roman province of Achaia (uh KAY yuh). The city was so well-known for its sexual immorality that a word meaning "to live like a Corinthian" meant to live immorally. Corinth is prominent in the New Testament because the New Testament contains not only the account of Paul's work in the Book of Acts but also two long letters from Paul to the Corinthian church.

Paul was alone when he arrived in Corinth. His two missionary associates—Silas (SIGH luhs) and Timothy—arrived only later (v. 5). Like all Jewish rabbis, Paul had a trade other than teaching; his was tentmaking. (Some Bible scholars think the word means "leatherworking.") Paul sought and found a tentmaker named Aquila in Corinth. Aquila invited Paul to stay with him and to work with him while he was in Corinth.

Luke tells us that Aquila was a Jew who had been born in Pontus, a region of Asia Minor. Before coming to Corinth, Aquila had lived in Italy. Aquila and his wife Priscilla were forced to leave Rome because Claudius Caesar expelled the Jews from Rome. Large groups of Jews lived throughout the Roman Empire, especially in the large cities. Since the expulsion of Jews by Claudius was between January 25, A.D. 49 and January 24, A.D. 50, we have a general idea of when Paul arrived in Corinth.

Acts 18:2–3 gives some basic facts about Aquila and Priscilla, but it doesn't answer all our questions. For example, "Was Priscilla also a Jew?" Some have theorized that she was a Roman who married the Jew Aquila. Although Jewish leaders frowned on such mixed marriages, we know that Timothy's mother married a Greek (Acts 16:3).

An even more important question is, "Were Aquila and Priscilla Christians before Paul met them?" The Book of Acts doesn't tell us, but there are reasons for thinking that they were already believers. For one thing, nothing is said of Paul witnessing to them as he did with Lydia (LID ih uh; Acts 16:14–15). Even more compelling is the reason given by a Roman historian for Claudius's expulsion order. The Jews were expelled because of a tumult instigated by one "Chrestus." Very likely, this means that the Jews were arguing about whether Jesus was the Christ. This shows that there were some Christians in Rome at an early date, and thus Acts 18:2 probably means that Aquila and Priscilla were among them.

If Aquila and Priscilla were already Christians, this explains why they so quickly opened their home and shared their work with Paul. It explains why Paul so quickly accepted their invitation. Using their home as a base and the tentmaking for financial support, Paul was able to launch his missionary campaign in Corinth. As usual, he began by going to the Jewish synagogue and preaching to Jews and God-fearing Gentiles.

II. In Ephesus (Acts 18:18–19, 24–26)

1. From Corinth to Ephesus (18:18–19)

18 And Paul after this tarried there yet a good while, and then took his leave of the brethren, and sailed thence into Syria, and with him Priscilla and Aquila; having shorn his head in Cenchrea [sen KREE uh]: for he had a vow.

19 And he came to Ephesus, and left them there: but he himself entered into the synagogue, and reasoned with the Jews.

The account of the rest of Paul's first visit to Corinth is in Acts 18:5–17. He endured many threats and had a vision that encouraged him to persevere. Paul left Corinth on his way eventually back to Syria, where the Antioch (AN tih ahk) church was. On the way, he stopped first at Cenchrea, near Corinth. Then he went to Ephesus for a short visit. From there he went to Caesarea, then to Jerusalem, and finally to Antioch (vv. 20–22).

When Paul was in Cenchrea, he cut off his hair as part of a Jewish vow. This was probably part of a vow that culminated in a visit to the temple when Paul was in Jerusalem. Acts 21:23–24 refers to a later visit to the temple to perform a vow. This shows that Paul considered himself a loyal Jew.

The first-century world was a mobile society. People moved about on the Roman system of roads and sailed on seas patrolled by Roman ships. One empire facilitated travel across provincial boundaries. We know that Paul spent much of his life on the road. Aquila and Priscilla provide another good example of mobility. Acts tells us that Aquila was from Pontus, that he and Priscilla lived in Rome, that they then moved to Corinth, and that they went with Paul to Ephesus. References in Paul's letters show that they remained for a while in Ephesus (1 Cor. 16:19), that later they were in Rome (Rom. 16:3–5), and that still later they returned to Ephesus (2 Tim. 4:19).

Like Abraham, this dedicated couple had a mobile faith. They did not confine their practice of the Christian faith to one locale. They took their faith with them. Wherever they lived was where they served the Lord.

2. Helping Apollos (18:24–26)

24 And a certain Jew named Apollos, born at Alexandria [al eg ZAN drih uh], an eloquent man, and mighty in the scriptures, came to Ephesus.

25 This man was instructed in the way of the Lord; and being fervent in the spirit, he spake and taught diligently the things of the Lord, knowing only the baptism of John.

26 And he began to speak boldly in the synagogue: whom when Aquila and Priscilla had heard, they took him unto them, and expounded unto him the way of God more perfectly.

Apollos was from Alexandria in Egypt. A large colony of Jews had lived there for centuries. Acts 18:24 shows that the Christian gospel had reached Alexandria by the middle of the first century. Apollos came from Alexandria to Ephesus and began to teach the things of the Lord. When he spoke in the synagogue, Aquila and Priscilla heard him. This shows that Jewish believers at this stage still worshiped with fellow Jews in the synagogue.

Aquila and Priscilla detected something lacking in what Apollos said. What was lacking? The description of Apollos before he met Aquila and Priscilla is impressive. He was eloquent and fervent. He knew the Scriptures and had been instructed in the way of the Lord. This enabled him to teach about Jesus. In spite of all these things, Apollos knew "only the baptism of John." This may mean that Apollos had not heard about the death and resurrection of Jesus. It may mean that he had not heard about Pentecost or experienced the fullness of the Spirit. It may mean that what Apollos taught about baptism was limited to John's baptism of repentance and did not include the picture of death and resurrection in Christian baptism.

Whatever it meant, Aquila and Priscilla were disturbed to hear a spokesman for Jesus not declare all that God had revealed. Under similar conditions, lesser people might have launched a campaign of criticism against Apollos. Instead, this dedicated couple quietly invited Apollos to meet with them, and they explained to him more completely the way of God. This took love, courage, and tact. Apollos accepted their instruction with openness, humility, and gratitude. As a result, Apollos went on to effective ministry (Acts 18:27–28; 1 Cor. 3:4–7).

III. In Rome (Rom. 16:3–5a)

3 Greet Priscilla and Aquila my helpers in Christ Jesus:
4 Who have for my life laid down their own necks: unto whom not only I give thanks, but also all the churches of the Gentiles.
5 Likewise greet the church that is in their house.

By the time Paul wrote to the church at Rome, Priscilla and Aquila were back in Rome. Paul paid tribute not only by calling them helpers in Christ Jesus but also by thanking God that they had risked their own lives for him. We don't know the circumstances when these friends risked their lives for Paul. Acts 19:28–41 describes a riot in Ephesus, in which Paul was in danger. Paul mentioned dangers in Ephesus in 1 Corinthians 15:32 and 16:9. Perhaps one of these was the occasion. Wherever it was, Paul clearly testified that Priscilla and Aquila had risked their own lives for him.

Paul greeted not only them but also the church in their house. According to 1 Corinthians 16:19, a church had also met in their house when they were in Ephesus. First-century churches did not have buildings of their own. They met in rented halls (Acts 19:9) and more often in private houses (Acts 2:46; 12:12; Philem. 2). One evidence of the commitment of Priscilla and Aquila is that they practiced their faith wherever they moved. This is evident because they opened their house as a meeting place for the churches in Ephesus and in Rome.

It is interesting to notice that all New Testament references to either Priscilla or Aquila always include both names. Also, the sequence of their names varies. Sometimes Aquila is listed first, and sometimes, Priscilla. (Her name is sometimes listed as Prisca, but most often as Priscilla.) These references show that this Christian couple not only shared life together but also participated jointly in their service to the Lord.

APPLYING THE BIBLE

1. Persecution spreads the gospel. God uses all things that befall us—both the good and the bad—to further His work. A case in point is the persecution of Aquila and Priscilla. They were Jews driven from their

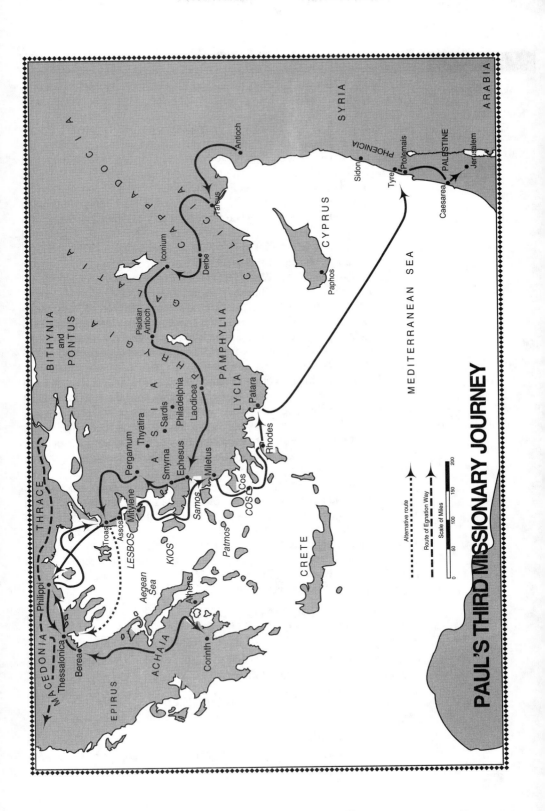

PAUL'S THIRD MISSIONARY JOURNEY

Alternative route

Route of Egnation Way

Scale of Miles

0   50   100   150   200

home in Rome by Emperor Claudius. According to the *Holman Bible Dictionary,* Claudius drove the Jews out of Rome in about A.D. 49 "probably due to a conflict between Jews and Christians in Rome"[1] (see also Acts 18:2). Claudius was probably poisoned by his fourth wife Aquippina "in A.D. 54 and [she] took charge of the empire for her son Nero"[2] But in human affairs, God always has the last word. Persecution of the Jews only served to spread the gospel more rapidly, for Aquila and Priscilla were forced to move to Corinth, where they met Paul (Acts 18:1–4).

2. God uses common folks. God often uses common people who do His work in the background. The ministry of Billy Graham has been unique and powerful, but no more important to God than that work of a faithful pastor in a country church who gives his all to Jesus. Aquila and Priscilla were simple tentmakers (v. 3) or leather workers. They worked with their hands, but they used their hands for God's glory.

3. Paul finds a home. When Paul moved from Athens to Corinth, he found an open door to the home of Aquila and Priscilla. Verse 3 says, "And because he was of the same craft, he abode with them." They probably worked as tentmakers in their own home. At least they offered Paul accommodations in their home and he lived and worked with them. How marvelously God works to care for His own, not only in spiritual blessings but in material blessings as well.

4. Taking the faith "on the road." Notice how much Paul moved about and how many cities he visited. Observe, too, the movements of Aquila and Priscilla who, like Paul, "took their faith on the road."

But the point is that the good news is tailored for the road. We are not to lock our faith up in some isolated cloister or closet at home. It is to be taken with us, following the example of Aquila and Priscilla, and shared with those we meet daily.

5. Tentmakers teach the teacher. When Apollos came to Ephesus, he began to teach in the synagogue, but Aquila and Priscilla readily saw that something was lacking. As our lesson points out very clearly, they took him aside and "expounded unto him the way of God more perfectly" (18:26). They did not criticize or embarrass him publicly. What gracious people they were; and, no doubt, this ministry to Apollos was one of their greatest contributions to the Christian faith because of Apollos's unique qualifications (18:24).

TEACHING THE BIBLE

▶ *Main Idea:* Christ calls us to share our faith wherever we go.

▶ *Suggested Teaching Aim:* To lead adults to identify ways they can serve Christ as they go about their daily work.

A TEACHING OUTLINE

1. Use thought questions to introduce the study.

2. Use small groups to examine the Bible passage or use the material with the whole class.

3. *Use discussion questions to examine how the Scripture applies to members' lives.*

4. *Use a listing of principles to help members apply the Bible study to their personal lives.*

Introduce the Bible Study

Ask: What do you think about a person who witnesses on the job? Should that person have a right to do so? Do you like to shop in a store where you know the person is a Christian? Would you more likely buy from a Christian business if you had a choice?

Suggest that today's lesson is about a husband and wife team who used their business to spread the gospel.

Search for Biblical Truth

Display the unit poster and point out the lesson for today. On three separate sheets of paper write one of the following cities: *Corinth, Ephesus,* and *Rome.* Place these at three places around the room.

If your class works well in groups, form three groups and assign each of them one of the cities. (You need not have more than one person in a group.) Ask them to read the biblical material about Priscilla and Aquila that relates to that city: Corinth—Acts 18:1–4; Ephesus—Acts 18:18–19, 24–26; Rome—Romans 16:3–5a. Ask them to answer the following questions: (1) Who is the passage about? (2) What did the people do? (3) How did this help spread the gospel? (4) What principles for living in today's world can you find in your passage? Either write these questions on a chalkboard or a large sheet of paper so all can see or make a copy for each of the three groups.

If your class does not work well in small groups, use the above four questions and ask members to work as a whole. Whether you work in groups or as a whole class, use the following discussion questions to help apply the Scripture after you have examined the Bible passage for each city.

Corinth: How do you think Priscilla and Aquila used their business to further Christianity? How can you use your business or job to further the cause of Christ? What should you do? What should you be careful to avoid? List the principles for living in today's world on a chalkboard or a large sheet of paper.

Ephesus: As you travel on vacations or business, how can you share your faith? What are some actions you could take? What should you avoid? Do you know someone who is immature in the faith whom you can help? Use "Studying the Bible" to explain the three possible meanings of "knowing only the baptism of John." List the principles for living in today's world on a chalkboard or a large sheet of paper.

Rome: How can you use your home to further the gospel of Christ? How willing are you to risk your "neck" (Rom. 16:4) to help someone who has taken a stand for Christ? List the principles for living in today's world on a chalkboard or a large sheet of paper.

Give the Truth a Personal Focus

Read over the list of principles for living in today's world and ask members if they would like to add any others to the list. Ask members to evaluate these principles to see which ones would apply to their lives. Ask them to choose at least one principle they will commit to put into practice. Distribute paper and pencils. Ask them to write this principle on the paper and keep it in their Bibles to remind them of it. Close with a prayer of commitment that members will follow through on the decisions they made.

---

1. *Holman Bible Dictionary*, s.v. "Claudius."
2. Ibid. 268.

Timothy

Basic Passages: Acts 16:1–5; 1 Corinthians 4:14–17; Philippians 2:19–24; 2 Timothy 1:3–7; 3:14–15

Focal Passages: Acts 16:1–5; 1 Corinthians 4:14–17; Philippians 2:19–22; 2 Timothy 1:4–7

Paul and Timothy served the Lord by serving each other and the churches. Paul was Timothy's father in the faith. He taught Timothy and gave him many opportunities for service. Timothy was Paul's helper, companion, and representative on many missions. The churches benefited from the work of these two partners in the gospel.

▶**Study Aim:** *To describe how Paul and Timothy helped each other and the churches*

STUDYING THE BIBLE

OUTLINE AND SUMMARY

    I. **Paul Invited Timothy to Go with Him (Acts 16:1–5)**

   II. **Paul Sent Timothy on Special Missions (1 Cor. 4:14–17; Phil. 2:19–24)**

      1. Mission to Corinth (1 Cor. 4:14–17)

      2. Mission to Philippi (Phil. 2:19–24)

  III. **Paul Challenged Timothy to Remain Faithful (2 Tim. 1:3–7; 3:14–15)**

      1. Remembering how he was raised (2 Tim. 1:3–5; 3:14–15)

      2. Stirring up the gift of God (2 Tim. 1:6–7)

Paul chose Timothy, a disciple living in Lystra (LISS truh), well spoken of by the believers, to join him on his missionary journey (Acts 16:1–5). Paul sent Timothy, his beloved and faithful son in the Lord, to remind the Corinthians of Paul's teachings about the Christian life (1 Cor. 4:14–17). In writing of his plans to send Timothy to Philippi (FILL ih pigh), Paul commended Timothy as one who cared for the Philippians and put the work of the Lord above his own interests (Phil. 2:19–24). In his final letter, Paul thanked God for the sincere faith of Timothy, his grandmother, and mother (2 Tim. 1:3–5; 3:14–15). Paul challenged Timothy to rekindle God's gift and to live in the courage of His Spirit (2 Tim. 1:6–7).

I. Paul Invited Timothy to Go with Him (Acts 16:1–5)

1 Then came he to Derbe [DIR bih] and Lystra: and, behold, a certain disciple was there, named Timotheus [tih MOH thih uhs], the son of a certain woman, which was a Jewess, and believed; but his father was a Greek:

2 Which was well reported of by the brethren that were at Lystra and Iconium [igh KOH nih uhm].

3 Him would Paul have to go forth with him; and took and circumcised him because of the Jews which were in those quarters: for they knew all that his father was a Greek.

4 And as they went through the cities, they delivered them the decrees for to keep, that were ordained of the apostles and elders which were at Jerusalem.

5 And so were the churches established in the faith, and increased in number daily.

On Paul's first missionary journey, he had preached in the cities mentioned in Acts 16:1–5 (Acts 14). Now he was returning in order to encourage the believers and strengthen the churches. While he was there, Paul also reported on the decisions of the Jerusalem Conference (Acts 15). Verse 5 shows the successful results of this return visit by Paul.

While he was in Lystra, Paul noticed a young disciple named Timothy. This young man had a good reputation in Lystra and in the neighboring town of Iconium. Paul was so impressed by Timothy that he invited him to join Paul and Silas in their missionary work. Thus began an association between Paul and Timothy that lasted throughout the rest of Paul's life.

Timothy probably had become a Christian during Paul's first visit to Lystra. His mother was a believing Jew. His father was a Greek; therefore, Timothy had not been circumcised. Paul circumcised Timothy because he was a Jew. Paul defended the principle that a Gentile believer need not be circumcised in order to follow Jesus; however, he recognized that circumcision was still proper for a Jew. If Timothy was not circumcised, he and Paul would encounter resistance in future work with fellow Jews.

II. Paul Sent Timothy on Special Missions (1 Cor. 4:14–17; Phil. 2:19–24)

1. Mission to Corinth (1 Cor. 4:14–17)

14 I write not these things to shame you, but as my beloved sons I warn you.

15 For though ye have ten thousand instructors in Christ, yet have ye not many fathers: for in Christ Jesus I have begotten you through the gospel.

16 Wherefore I beseech you, be ye followers of me.

17 For this cause have I sent unto you Timotheus, who is my beloved son, and faithful in the Lord, who shall bring you into remembrance of my ways, which be in Christ, as I teach every where in every church.

In the early chapters of 1 Corinthians, Paul rebuked the church at Corinth for their selfish pride and disruptive dissension. Paul contrasted their selfishness with the sacrifices of the apostles (1 Cor. 4:10–13). He explained that his purpose was not to shame them but to admonish them as a father does his children. They might have many teachers in the Christian life, but they had only one spiritual father. Paul referred to himself as their father because he was the one who brought the gospel to them and first taught them how to live as Christians (Acts 18:1–17). He was not seeking to replace God as their Father. He and they had a distinctive relationship that enabled him to speak to them as a father.

Verse 16 is not evidence of Paul's arrogance. The ancient world was a sinful place. Most Gentiles had no background in the moral teachings of Judaism. They needed to learn how to live as Christians. The missionaries taught them by their words and by their own example.

Timothy had been with Paul during much of his initial work in Corinth (Acts 18:5). Paul sent Timothy on many special missions (Acts 17:14–15; 18:5; 19:22; 1 Thess. 3:2, 6). Paul sent Timothy to Corinth on just such a mission. Paul himself planned to come soon to deal with the situation in Corinth (1 Cor. 4:18–19). In the meanwhile, he sent Timothy.

Paul commended Timothy as his beloved son, probably referring to Paul's part in Timothy's conversion and certainly referring to Paul's role as teacher and mentor. Paul also commended Timothy's faithfulness in the Lord. Paul trusted Timothy to remind the Corinthians of what Paul taught in all the churches about how to live as Christians in a non-Christian world.

2. Mission to Philippi (Phil. 2:19–24)

19 But I trust in the Lord Jesus to send Timotheus shortly unto you, that I also may be of good comfort, when I know your state.

20 For I have no man likeminded, who will naturally care for your state.

21 For all seek their own, not the things which are Jesus Christ's.

22 But ye know the proof of him, that, as a son with the father, he hath served with me in the gospel.

Paul was under arrest in Rome when he wrote the Philippian church. He wrote to testify to his joy in the Lord and to express gratitude for their partnership in the gospel. Paul's letter also shows that he saw signs of the kind of selfish pride that led to disruptive dissension in Corinth (Phil. 2:14; 4:2). Thus he challenged them to practice the kind of self-giving love perfectly exemplified in Jesus Christ (2:1–11). Then Paul gave some human examples of unselfish commitment to Christ. He mentioned himself (2:14–18), Timothy (2:19–24), and Epaphroditus (ih PAF roh DIGH tuhs) (2:25–30). Thus although on the surface Philippians 2:19–24 reads like travel plans, Paul had a more serious purpose.

Paul's commendation of Timothy in these verses is unsurpassed. No person was so like-minded to Paul as Timothy. He had for the Philippians the same deep concern as Paul had. Timothy had been with Paul when he answered the Macedonian call and went to Philippi (Acts 16). The Philippians knew of Timothy's relation with Paul and of his untiring work on behalf of the cause of Christ. In a self-seeking world, a spirit that too often invades Christian ranks, Timothy stood out as one who sought not his own interests; instead he sought the things of the Lord.

Like a son with a father, Timothy had served with Paul as a partner in the gospel. They both claimed the title "slaves" of Christ. They served their Master by serving the churches. As they did, their effectiveness was enhanced by their service to each other. Paul planned to send Timothy to Philippi, but for the time being he needed Timothy with him (v. 23). Paul hoped eventually to be set free and to visit Philippi himself (v. 24).

III. Paul Challenged Timothy to Remain Faithful (2 Tim. 1:3–7; 3:14–15)

1. Remembering how he was raised (2 Tim. 1:3–5; 3:14–15)

4 Greatly desiring to see thee, being mindful of thy tears, that I may be filled with joy;

5 When I call to remembrance the unfeigned faith that is in thee, which dwelt first in thy grandmother Lois, and thy mother Eunice [YOO niss]; and I am persuaded that in thee also.

Paul's final letter was to Timothy. Paul thanked God that Timothy was in his thoughts day and night (1:3). Later in the letter, Paul urged Timothy to come to him quickly (4:9). Paul was in prison again and knew that his death was near (4:6–8).

Although he faced death unafraid, he wanted to see Timothy one last time. Paul knew of Timothy's deep concern for him, and he hoped for the joy of seeing him again.

Paul paid tribute to the genuine faith of Timothy, a faith without any insincerity or hypocrisy. Paul reminded Timothy that this was the kind of faith his grandmother and mother had. Paul was sure Timothy had the same kind of faith. Lois and Eunice had been loyal Jews who believed in God as revealed in the Old Testament Scriptures. We don't know at what point Lois and Eunice became believers in Christ. Paul said that they were believers before Timothy was. They certainly taught Timothy the Scriptures when he was a child (2 Tim. 3:14–15). This knowledge of the Bible was the foundation for Timothy's own faith.

2. Stirring up the gift of God (2 Tim. 1:6–7)

6 Wherefore I put thee in remembrance that thou stir up the gift of God, which is in thee by the putting on of my hands.

7 For God hath not given us the spirit of fear; but of power, and of love, and of a sound mind.

Paul reminded Timothy that God had endowed him with a gift. Paul himself had laid his hands on Timothy in prayerful dedication of Timothy to faithfully use the gift entrusted to him. The apostle challenged Timothy to rekindle the gift as one stirs the coals of fire to keep it burning.

Then Paul reminded Timothy that God's Spirit does not produce fear. Instead God's Spirit imparts power, love, and self-discipline (the likely meaning of the word translated "sound mind"). Do these reminders indicate that Paul recognized in Timothy a timid spirit that might falter in the face of the worst kind of persecution? The same question might be asked about verse 8, where Paul challenged Timothy not to be ashamed of the Lord or of Paul, His prisoner. Some Bible students think such timidity is implied by Paul's famous challenge to Timothy: "Let no man despise thy youth" (1 Tim. 4:12).

Another explanation for Paul's challenges is that every believer is human enough at times to be tempted to falter in the face of dangers and threats. Who is there who hasn't felt some fears about giving a bold testimony for Christ? Paul's words, therefore, may not imply any perceived weakness in Timothy other than what afflicts all believers. All of us need to be reminded to stir up the gift of God. All of us need to remember that God gave us a Spirit of power, not of fear.

APPLYING THE LESSON

1. No such thing as a bad boy. Some of us grew up knowing about Father Joseph Flanagan, who founded Boys Town in Omaha, Nebraska, in 1917. He took in boys brought before the courts and gave them a second chance. Flanagan's motto was, "There is no such thing as a bad boy." He is remembered for a picture of a boy about ten or eleven years old carrying a smaller boy on his back. Beneath the picture are the words: "He's not heavy; he's my brother."

Paul met a youth named Timothy who was reared in a godly home, took him under his wing, and taught him. God used Timothy mightily in His service. Paul carried Timothy in his heart and was the making of the young preacher (Acts 16:1–5; 2 Tim. 1:5–6).

2. The best time of life. Someone has said, "Youth is the best time of life." But Robert Browning wrote: "Grow old along with me! The best is yet to be." Really, today is the best time of life, for it is all of life we have! But a great deal can be said about the advantages of youth.

George Bernard Shaw once said that youth is so wonderful that "it's too bad to waste it on young people!" Timothy was young when he met Paul, and that was the turning point in life for Timothy. They first met on Paul's first missionary journey. The good seed had already been planted in Timothy's heart at home (1:3–5). Paul said Timothy was "my beloved son" in the gospel (1 Cor. 4:17). It was the combination of Lois, Eunice, and Paul's witness that brought the youth to Jesus. Now Timothy was ready for the Master's finishing touches which he would learn from Paul (1 Cor. 4:15–17; 2 Tim. 1:6–7).

The best time in life to come to the Savior is when we are young and have all our life to give Him (see Eccles. 12:1). Fortunately, that has been the experience of many of us.

3. Timid Timothy? I have always thought of Timothy, at least in his early ministry, as being timid and unsure of himself. Perhaps it came from the strong influence of his mother and grandmother, for nothing is said of his father except he was a Greek. Was Timothy's timidity the reason Paul wrote the words found in 2 Tim. 1:6–7? Paul knew what was in Timothy and he knew it needed to be "stirred up" and shared courageously.

Many failures come to us because we lack confidence. We fear being inferior. More failures result from our lack of confidence than from our lack of ability. Some of us have had to wrestle hard with this problem that, somehow, was rooted in our early years. But Paul helped Timothy work through it, and Paul was able to write about his young son in the ministry the glowing recommendation of Philippians 2:19–24.

4. Three indispensable elements for the ministry. In 1 Corinthians 13:13, Paul lists three indispensable virtues for effective Christian living. In 2 Timothy 1:6–7, he lists three "indispensables" for the Christian minister: power, love, and a sound mind.

(1) *Power.* The Greek word for power gives us our English word *dynamite.* Kenneth Wuest says this was the force of character Timothy needed which—since apparently not natural to Timothy—could be inspired by the consciousness of a divine call.

(2) *Love.* This is not softness. It is the Greek word *agape,* which describes divine love that bestows itself freely without any thought of return. It is the fruit of the Spirit (Gal. 5:22).

(3) *Sound mind.* Wuest describes this indispensable quality as self-discipline, which is opposed to all easy self-indulgence that produces laxity. These three indispensable qualities every young minister needs are leadership, love, and self-control. They go together. Without any one of them trouble lies ahead for the aspiring young preacher.

TEACHING THE BIBLE

▶ *Main Idea:* All of us have the ability to affirm those who have helped us in the faith.

▶ *Suggested Teaching Aim:* To express thanks to those who have been our spiritual teachers.

A TEACHING OUTLINE

1. Use testimonies to introduce the Bible study.

2. Use brief lectures and group discussion to guide the Bible study.

3. Use letter writing to make the Bible study personal.

Introduce the Bible Study

Ask members to describe the person who has helped them most in their spiritual lives. If you know of special relationships in the class where mature Christians have helped new believers, contact the new believers **IN ADVANCE** and ask them to be ready to express how the mature Christians helped them.

Point out the lesson title on the unit poster and suggest that Paul and Timothy had a special relationship that lasted as long as Paul lived.

Search for Biblical Truth

IN ADVANCE, ask a member to read aloud the Scripture passages as you study them. Call for the reader to read Acts 16:1–5. Use a brief lecture to cover the following points in "Studying the Bible": (1) Timothy's Jewish-Greek background; (2) why Paul invited Timothy to join with him and Silas; (3) why Paul circumcised Timothy; (4) what was the result of their ministry.

DISCUSS: How do we know when we are violating some eternal principle or are helping to further the gospel by compromising some of our beliefs?

Call for the reader to read 1 Corinthians 4:14–17. Use a brief lecture to cover the following points in "Studying the Bible": (1) the situation at Corinth; (2) Paul's relationship to the Corinthians; (3) what Paul hoped would happen in Corinth; (4) Paul's relationship with Timothy.

DISCUSS: How do we know either as parents or spiritual parents when to correct and when to let our offspring make their own mistakes?

Call for the reader to read Philippians 2:19–22. Use a brief lecture to cover the following points in "Studying the Bible": (1) where Paul was when he wrote this; (2) why Paul wrote Philippians; (3) Paul's high estimation of Timothy; (4) Paul and Timothy's father-son spiritual relationship.

DISCUSS: How does a spiritual relationship increase the depth of friendship?

Call for the reader to read 2 Timothy 1:4–5. Use a brief lecture to cover the following points in "Studying the Bible": (1) where Paul was when he wrote this letter; (2) Paul's great love for Timothy; (3) the influence of Timothy's home life on his spiritual life.

DISCUSS: What steps can parents take to assure the spiritual growth of their children? Or can they assure it?

Call for the reader to read 2 Timothy 1:6–7. Use a brief lecture to cover the following points in "Studying the Bible": (1) Paul's reminder that God had gifted Timothy; (2) Paul's challenge to Timothy to stir up his commitment to God; (3) Paul's emphasis on power, love, and self-discipline instead of fearfulness.

DISCUSS: What helps you to rekindle your faith when you grow cold spiritually? How have others helped you at this point?

If you choose not to lecture you can use these questions in at least two other ways. Form five small groups and give each group a set of the questions to answer or you can ask the questions as a group activity. In some cases, you may have to supply the information because members will not have the information you have.

Give the Truth a Personal Focus

Distribute paper, envelopes, and pencils and ask members to write a letter to someone who has helped them grow spiritually. Ask members to mail the letter this week.

Proclaim the Gospel!

Basic Passage: 1 Thessalonians 2:1–13

Focal Passage: 1 Thessalonians 2:1–13

Paul's two letters to the believers at Thessalonica (THESS uh loh NIGH kuh) were the earliest of his New Testament letters. (Some date Galatians earlier.) He wrote 1 Thessalonians (thess uh LOH nih uhns) not long after his missionary work there (Acts 17:1–9). Paul wrote to encourage new converts and to deal with some issues that had arisen since his visit. One of his purposes was to counteract false perceptions of the proclamation of the gospel by Paul and his companions.

▶**Study Aim:** *To recognize how Paul dealt with perceptions of false motives and methods in proclaiming the gospel*

STUDYING THE BIBLE

OUTLINE AND SUMMARY

  I. **Motives and Methods for Proclaiming the Gospel (1 Thess. 2:1–12)**
  1. Courage in face of opposition (vv. 1–2)
  2. Not error, immorality, or guile (vv. 3–4)
  3. Not flattery, greed, or pride (vv. 5–6)
  4 Gentle and self-giving (vv. 7–8)
  5. Hardworking and morally blameless (vv. 9–10)
  6. Fatherly exhortation to worthy living (vv. 11–12)
 II. **Welcoming the Word of God (1 Thess. 2:13)**

In spite of being opposed in Philippi, Paul and his companions went on to Thessalonica, prepared to boldly face further contention (vv. 1–2). They did not practice false teaching, unclean living, or deceit, but were faithful stewards of the gospel (vv. 3–4). They did not practice flattery, nor were they motivated by desire for money or glory (vv. 5–6). They were gentle as a nursing mother and self-giving rather than self-serving (vv. 7–8). They worked to support themselves and practiced what they preached in godly living (vv. 9–10). Like a father does his children, they exhorted and encouraged each Thessalonian believer to live a life worthy of the God who called them (vv. 11–12). Paul thanked God that the Thessalonians had welcomed the missionaries' words as the word of God, not of men (v. 13).

I. Motives and Methods for Proclaiming the Gospel (1 Thess. 2:1–12)

1. Courage in face of opposition (vv. 1–2)

1 For yourselves, brethren, know our entrance in unto you, that it was not in vain.

2 But even after that we had suffered before, and were shamefully entreated, as ye know, at Philippi [FIL ih pigh],

we were bold in our God to speak unto you the gospel of God with much contention.

Verses 1–12 were written to defend Paul against certain false charges or perceptions. Acts 17:5–14 show that Paul had aroused strong opposition. It was strong enough to drive him out of town and even out of the next town. After he left, his enemies may have tried to undermine Paul by attributing certain false motives to him. Traveling religious teachers were common in the first-century world. Many of them were little more than con men using religion for their own selfish purposes. The apostle wanted to head off any comparison to these religious hucksters.

In chapter 1, Paul thanked God for the genuine faith of the Thessalonians (vv. 3–4). God's Spirit had used the missionaries' proclamation to lead many to follow the Lord (vv. 5–6). They had become examples throughout the entire region (vv. 7–10). Paul continued this theme in 1 Thessalonians 2:1. No one knew better than the Thessalonians that the work of Paul among them had not been in vain.

Then Paul reminded them of the opposition he and his companions had faced in order to preach in Thessalonica. Just before going there, Paul had been falsely accused, beaten, and imprisoned in Philippi. He was shamefully treated although he was a Roman citizen (Acts 16:12–40). When Paul reached Thessalonica, he and his friends were subject to further opposition and humiliation at the hands of enemies of the gospel.

Paul's point is that the missionaries were not defeated by such opposition. They persevered boldly in spite of it. A charlatan would never have faced what Paul boldly faced.

2. Not error, immorality, or guile (vv. 3–4)

> **3 For our exhortation was not of deceit, nor of uncleanness, nor in guile:**

Verse 3 lists three charges or false perceptions: error, immorality, and guile. The word translated "deceit" is a word from which we get our word *planet*. Because ancient people thought of planets as wandering and erratic, the word carried the idea of "error." Paul flatly denied that he was guilty of false teachings. The word "uncleanness" referred to moral uncleanness. Sexual immorality was a plague in many cities of the Roman Empire. Traveling preachers were often guilty of either promoting sexual sins or secretly committing such sins. The word "guile" referred to the use of underhanded methods to gain followers. Itinerant religious preachers were skilled in the art of persuading people by using various tricks and manipulation.

> **4 But as we were allowed of God to be put in trust with the gospel, even so we speak; not as pleasing men, but God, which trieth out hearts.**

Paul not only denied that he had used such methods, but he also stated the truth about his proclamation. The missionaries had been entrusted by God with the gospel. He had entrusted it to them because He had tested and proved them. The words "allowed" and "tried" translate the same word, which means "approved after passing the test." Because they viewed the gospel as entrusted to them by God, their goal was to please God, not to please people.

3. Not flattery, greed, or pride (vv. 5–6)

> **5 For neither at any time used we flattering words, as ye know, nor a cloak of covetousness; God is witness:**

> **6 Nor of men sought we glory, neither of you, nor yet of others, when we might have been burdensome, as the apostles of Christ.**

Verses 5–6 reflect three other charges or false perceptions. Paul denied that the missionaries had used flattery. This charge is closely related to the idea of using guile. Flattery is one of the tools of a con man. Paul reminded the Thessalonians that they themselves well knew that the missionaries didn't resort to flattery to gain a following.

Paul also denied that he and his associates were guilty of another besetting sin of traveling preachers: covetousness. Such religious hucksters used religion to make money for themselves. Paul said that God was witness to the fact that the missionaries were not in it for the money.

Religious leaders often gain a certain amount of praise from their followers. A worldly spirit feeds on such worldly praise. Some who proclaim the gospel successfully are tempted to forget what Jesus said about true greatness (Mark 10:35–45). Paul denied that he sought glory either from the Thessalonians or from others. The word translated "burdensome" means "weight." It can mean a burden or a weighty, important person. Thus Paul might have been saying that the apostles could have expected financial support, but Paul refused it from the Thessalonians. Or he could have been reminding them that the apostles could have expected praise and honor as weighty men, but chose to follow the Lord's example of humble service.

4. Gentle and self-giving (vv. 7–8)

> **7 But we were gentle among you, even as a nurse cherisheth her children:**

> **8 So being affectionately desirous of you, we were willing to have imparted unto you, not the gospel of God only, but also our own souls, because ye were dear unto us.**

Verses 7–8 stress the love of Paul and the others for the Thessalonians. Rather than being self-serving charlatans, they were self-giving servants. This theme is set forth in several ways. Verse 7 describes their love for the Thessalonians as being gentle, like that of a nurse or nursing mother. Some translators think the context and meaning of the word favor "nursing mother" rather than "nurse." In either case, the picture is one of gentleness, nurture, and love.

Verse 8 is filled with words of similar meaning. Paul spoke of affection for them. Because of such love, the missionaries shared the good news of God with them. However, they didn't stop with sharing the gospel; they also shared themselves because the Thessalonians were dear to them. The word "dear" is an adjective connected with the word *agape*.

5. Hardworking and morally blameless (vv. 9–10)

9 For ye remember, brethren, our labour and travail: for labouring night and day, because we would not be chargeable unto any of you, we preached unto you the gospel of God.

Paul refused to accept money from the people of Thessalonica. In Corinth, he followed a similar policy, which he explained in 1 Corinthians 9 (see also 2 Thess. 3:9). Paul claimed that preachers had a right to expect to be paid; however, Paul voluntarily refused pay at places where he thought accepting money could be used by his opponents to attack Paul and his message. Paul did accept money from the Philippians, some of it even when he was in Thessalonica (Phil. 4:10–19). However, Paul often worked, apparently at tentmaking (Acts 18:3), in order not to provide any grounds for criticism about money.

Paul reminded the Thessalonians of this fact in verse 9. He had worked night and day both earning his living and telling the good news of God. No one could accuse Paul of being greedy or lazy.

10 Ye are witnesses, and God also, how holily and justly and unblameably we behaved ourselves among you that believe:

Paul reminded his readers that the missionaries practiced what they preached. Nothing so undermines a preacher's credibility as committing the sins he condemns. Paul used three words to emphasize the godly example of the missionaries: holy, righteous, and blameless. They lived as people set apart by God and for God. They did what was right. Their lives were above reproach. No one could rightly accuse them of sinful living.

As in verse 5, Paul cited two witnesses of the truth of what he wrote. The believers in Thessalonica were witnesses, and God Himself was a witness on their behalf.

6. Fatherly exhortation to worthy living (vv. 11–12)

11 As ye know how we exhorted and comforted and charged every one of you, as a father doth his children,

12 That ye would walk worthy of God, who hath called you unto his kingdom and glory.

In verse 8, Paul had compared the missionaries' love to the gentle love of a mother for her children. In verse 11, he compared their love to the firm but encouraging love of a father for his children. Just as a father exhorts and encourages each of his children to live worthily of his name and upbringing, Paul exhorted the believers to walk worthily of the divine calling (see Eph. 4:1). Children of God are citizens of an eternal kingdom. We live in a world that is governed by worldly values, but we are expected to live worthily of God's kingdom.

II. Welcoming the Word of God (1 Thess. 2:13)

13 For this cause also thank we God without ceasing, because, when ye received the word of God which ye heard of us, ye received it not as the word of men, but as it is in truth, the word of God, which effectually worketh in you that believe.

The second word translated "received" carries the idea of welcoming the word of God. The Greek word is the usual one for the reception of a guest. Outwardly receiving the word is comparable to hearing it. Inwardly receiving it takes place when the hearer accepts and welcomes it. Paul expressed continual gratitude to God that the Thessalonians accepted the words of the missionaries as much more than the words of some traveling preachers. They welcomed the words as the word of God, which indeed it was. This same word continues its work in the lives of those who believe.

APPLYING THE BIBLE

1. The importance of encouragement. After the end of the Civil War, General Robert E. Lee was named president of Washington College in Virginia. In one of his classes there was a poor boy who worked for a farmer several miles away and walked to class each day. Lee noticed the tired look on the boy's face and knew he was working hard on the farm and staying up late at night to study. One day Lee asked the boy what he did between classes, and the boy replied that he looked for an empty classroom that was warm.

"Don't do that," said the general. "Come to my office and sit. It's warm and I am seldom there."

Lee helped the boy get a job as a schoolteacher when he graduated, and his lifelong ambition was to be as kind and encouraging to others as Lee had been to him.

Our lesson writer points out that Paul wrote the new converts at Thessalonica to encourage them in the faith. Encouragement is one thing everyone needs, and each of us can give it to others.

2. Courage needed. When a Virginia plantation owner named George Washington took command of 13,743 "rebels," they were a motley crew. They had old weapons and no training. They were farmers dressed in tattered clothing, but he molded them into the Continental Army that defended their homeland and freed America from Britain's tyranny. Washington and his army did it through sheer force of will and fierce courage.

Paul cites the courage he exerted amid strong, satanic opposition, and uses it to stir up the courage of his readers to live for Jesus where it was so costly (vv. 1–2).

3. Kindness pays off. In his book *A Dictionary of Illustrations*, James Hefley tells about a traveler from New Jersey who stopped one Sunday to attend the worship services of the Methodist Church in Andersonville, Georgia. He never forgot the kindness that was shown to a stranger. When that stranger, Robert B. Brown, died at ninety, he left his entire estate, $178,302, to the Andersonville church. Kindness always pays off!

Paul reminds the Thessalonians how kindly and gently, "even as a nurse," he had ministered to them (vv.7–8). Surely, his example was an encouragement to them to treat others in the church the same way.

4. "The world has yet to see . . ." Dwight L. Moody, the well-known evangelist of the last century, was visiting one day in England with a man named Henry Varley. In the course of their conversation, Varley said:

"Moody, the world has yet to see what God will do with a man fully consecrated to Him."

Moody later confessed to Varley that those words became the driving force in his life. Before his death, Moody preached to more than a million people in America and England; and God used him to bring thousands to Christ.

This was also the driving force in Paul's life; and, surely, he came as close to it as any person who has ever lived (vv. 9–12).

TEACHING THE BIBLE

▶ **Main Idea:** Facing problems head-on is the best way to correct false accusations and charges.

▶ **Suggested Teaching Aim:** To lead adults to use gentleness and self-giving—not such methods as flattery and greed—to proclaim the gospel.

A TEACHING OUTLINE

1. Use a thought question to introduce the lesson.
2. Use two readers to help you with the lesson.
3. Use a poster to identify Paul's motives and methods for proclaiming the gospel.
4. Use summarizing to apply the Scripture to life.

Introduce the Bible Study

Ask members what motives the world attributes to many of the television and radio evangelists. Ask: Why do they do that? What could be done to change this attitude?

Search for Biblical Truth

Write on a chalkboard or a large sheet of paper:

"Motives and Methods for Proclaiming the Gospel"	
Positive	Negative

IN ADVANCE, enlist a member to read aloud the Scripture passages. Also, enlist a reader to read the summary statements in the outline and summary that correspond to the appropriate Scripture. Call for 2:1–2 and the corresponding summary statements to be read.

On a map locate Thessalonica and Philippi. In a brief lecture make the following points: (1) Verses 1–12 were written to defend Paul against certain false charges; (2) briefly summarize Acts 16:12–40 and 17:5–14 to show Paul's treatment at Philippi and Thessalonica; (3) the missionaries were not defeated by such opposition; a charlatan would not have faced what Paul boldly faced; (4) the missionaries demonstrated courage in face of opposition. Under "Positive" on the poster write *Courage in face of opposition.*

Call for 2:3–6 and the corresponding summary statements to be read. Say: Apparently three charges had been made against Paul by the Jews in Thessalonica after the missionaries had been run out of town. Paul denied that his teachings had contained any of these. What were the three charges listed in verse 3? (Error, immorality, and guile.) Use "Studying the Bible" to explain the three words. Ask: Why had God allowed this persecution to happen to faithful missionaries? (To test them to see if they were worthy to be entrusted with the gospel.) Ask: What three further charges did Paul deny in verses 5–6? (Flattery, covetousness, glory.) Use "Studying the Bible" to explain these three terms. Under "Negative" on the poster write *not error, immorality, guile, flattery, greed, pride.*

Call for 2:7–10 and the corresponding summary statements to be read. Ask members to look at these verses and to identify the positive reasons Paul and the missionaries shared the gospel with the Thessalonians. (Gentle, self-giving, love, hardworking, morally blameless, holy, righteous, and blameless.) Write these under "Positive" on the poster. Ask: Who did Paul call as witnesses to the missionaries' proper motives and behavior? (The believers in Thessalonica and God Himself.)

Call for 2:11–12 and the corresponding summary statement to be read. Ask: What was the goal of Paul's preaching to the Thessalonians? (Urging them to worthy living.) Under "Positive" write *Worthy living.*

Call for 2:13 and the corresponding summary statement to be read. Ask members to look at this verse to determine how the Thessalonians received the gospel the missionaries had preached. (As word of God, not word of men.)

Give the Truth a Personal Focus

Briefly review the poster and the positive and negative reasons for proclaiming the gospel. Ask members to write a one-sentence statement that would summarize the meaning of this passage for today. Let members develop their own statement, but consider this: *When believers face opposition to the gospel, they should not use such methods as flattery and greed but gentleness and self-giving to counteract the opposition.* Close with a prayer that members will be able to put this lesson into practice this week.

Live in Love and Holiness

Basic Passage: 1 Thessalonians 3:6–4:12

Focal Passage: 1 Thessalonians 3:12–4:12

Early Christian missionaries obeyed the Great Commission by teaching new converts the things Jesus had commanded (Matt. 28:18–20). The teachings stressed relationships and character. The new converts were taught how to love one another and all people. They were taught how to live as people set apart by God and for God. An example of this twofold emphasis is found in 1 Thessalonians 3:6–4:12.

▶**Study Aim:** *To state what Paul taught about expressing love and holiness*

STUDYING THE BIBLE

OUTLINE AND SUMMARY

  I. Paul's Relations with the Thessalonians (1 Thess. 3:6–13)

      1. Good news about the Thessalonians (vv. 6–10)

      2. Paul's prayer (vv. 11–13)

 II. Exhortations About Christian Living (1 Thess. 4:1–12)

      1. Growth in Christian living (vv. 1–2)

      2. Set apart from sexual sins (vv. 3–8)

      3. Growth in love (vv. 9–10)

      4. Necessity for work (vv. 11–12)

Paul rejoiced at the good news Timothy brought about the faith and love of the Thessalonians (3:6–10). He prayed that they might grow in love and holiness (3:11–13). He exhorted them to live according to the teachings of Jesus (4:1–2). He told them to abstain from sexual immorality because that was God's will, and he warned that committing such sins hurt people and would cause them to face God's wrath (4:3–8). Paul commended them for their love for one another and urged them to grow in such love (4:9–10). He repeated his earlier teachings to mind their own business and to do their own work (4:11–12).

I. Paul's Relations with the Thessalonians (1 Thess. 3:6–13)

1. Good news about the Thessalonians (vv. 6–10)

After leaving Thessalonica (THESS uh loh NIGH kuh), Paul was concerned about how well the church was enduring persecution (2:14). Therefore, he sent Timothy to bring him a report on the church (3:1–5). Paul rejoiced when Timothy brought good news about their faith and love (3:6). He was comforted by knowing they stood fast in the Lord (3:7–8). Paul could not thank God enough for his joy (3:9). He prayed continually that he might see them again and supply whatever was lacking in their faith (3:10).

2. Paul's prayer (vv. 11–13)

12 And the Lord make you to increase and abound in love one toward another, and toward all men, even as we do toward you:

13 To the end he may stablish your hearts unblameable in holiness before God, even our Father, at the coming of our Lord Jesus Christ with all his saints.

Paul asked God the Father and the Lord Jesus Christ to direct his way again to Thessalonica (v. 11). He also prayed that the Lord would cause them to grow in love—both to one another and to all people. Paul's prayer thus reflects the teaching of Jesus about love. Jesus stressed love for one another (John 13:34–35), but He also taught love for all people—neighbors and even enemies (Luke 10:25–37; Matt. 5:43–47).

Such abounding love would lead to inner stability with the final result that they would fulfill the purpose of being set apart by God. Several English words are translations of words from the same root word in Greek. The basic word means to be set apart by God and for God. The word "holy" describes those who have been set apart. So does the word "saints," which literally means "holy ones." "Sanctified" means "set apart." "Sanctification" is the process that results from being set apart. "Holiness" is the state resulting from being set apart. Believers are set apart at conversion and are called and empowered for a life that pleases God—one characterized by righteousness and purity.

Paul prayed that they would stand blameless before the Lord at His coming. They would stand in that holiness which was the result of God's work in their lives.

II. Exhortations About Christian Living
(1 Thess. 4:1–12)

The first three chapters dealt with a review of Paul's relations with the Thessalonians. Then Paul turned to a variety of issues about Christian living and doctrine. Some of the issues are more specific than others. Some issues may have been matters of concern about the Thessalonian church that Timothy reported to Paul. Some may simply have been teachings needed by all new converts in the first-century world.

1. Growth in Christian living (vv. 1–2)

1 Furthermore then we beseech you, brethren, and exhort you by the Lord Jesus, that as ye have received of us how ye ought to walk and to please God, so ye would abound more and more.

2 For ye know what commandments we gave you by the Lord Jesus.

Verse 1 begins a new section of Paul's letter. Paul began with a general exhortation to walk or live in accordance with what they had been taught by the missionaries. These teachings in turn had come from Jesus Himself. No doubt the life and teachings of Jesus formed the crux of what the apostles taught to new converts, just as the Cross and Resurrection formed the heart of the good news they preached to unbelievers (see 1 Cor. 7:10; 15:1–4). Paul acknowledged that they were already doing this, but he urged them to do so more and more.

2. Set apart from sexual sins (vv. 3–8)

3 For this is the will of God, even your sanctification, that ye should abstain from fornication:

Some areas of God's will must be sought diligently, but other areas are crystal clear. One such area is God's clear will that His children be set apart by God and for God. In verse 3, Paul focused on one specific aspect of holy living. Christians are to abstain from sexual immorality. The word "fornication" includes not only adultery but also sexual relations with anyone who is not one's spouse.

Was Paul aware of some specific problem in Thessalonica, as he was at Corinth (1 Cor. 5–6)? More likely, Paul was writing because he knew that the ancient world was riddled with sexual immorality. All kinds of sexual sins were widely practiced and condoned; some were even advocated as part of some religion. Also remember that Paul was writing from Corinth, which was noted as a sexual wilderness. Paul knew that many Gentile converts came from and still lived in such an environment. He wanted believers to know what the Lord expected in this key area of life.

4 That every one of you should know how to possess his vessel in sanctification and honour;

5 Not in the lust of concupiscence, even as the Gentiles which know not God:

Bible scholars debate the meaning of the word "vessel." Some believe that Paul was referring to the "body"; while others think Paul meant "wife." Those who think he meant "wife" also translate "possess" as "acquire." Thus the idea would be that Christian marriage makes far higher demands on men than the pagan double standard of sexual freedom for men. God demands lifetime loyalty to one woman in the one-flesh union of marriage.

If "vessel" meant "body," Paul was saying much the same thing as in 1 Corinthians 6:12–20. One's body is not for sexual immorality but is the temple of the Holy Spirit. For some, like Paul, this means to remain single; but for most it means Christian marriage (1 Cor. 7). Such marriage is only in the Lord (1 Cor. 7:39–40). It involves a mutual respect for each other within the one-flesh union of marriage (Gen. 2:24; 1 Cor. 7:2–5; Eph. 5:22–33).

The Bible teaches and the early missionaries stressed a Christian view of sex and marriage that ran counter to pagan practice. The practice of the non-Christian Gentile world is set forth in Romans 1:21–32. Christ calls for abstinence from sex before marriage and absolute faithfulness after marriage (see Matt. 19:1–12).

6 That no man go beyond and defraud his brother in any matter: because that the Lord is the avenger of all such, as we also have forewarned you and testified.

7 For God hath not called us unto uncleanness, but unto holiness.

8 He therefore that despiseth, despiseth not man, but God, who hath also given unto us his holy Spirit.

Many people today do not regard sexual immorality as sinful. Paul gave two reasons why it is. For one thing, sexual sin hurts people. Paul warned that it transgressed and defrauded one's brother. He probably used "brother" here more broadly than a man whose wife has been seduced into committing adultery. Paul surely included such an evil result; but he also included the harm done to the woman, her children, and many others touched by the sin. People sometimes try to excuse their sin by saying, "I'm hurting no one but myself." This is never true of sexual sins.

The second reason why sex outside marriage is wrong is because it ultimately is a sin against God. When David confessed his great sins, he prayed, "Against thee, thee only have I sinned, and done this evil in thy sight" (Ps. 51:4). David was not discounting the terrible harm of his sin to Uriah (yoo RIGH uh), Bathsheba (bath SHEE buh), and many others; but he was aware that the worst thing was that he had sinned against God. Paul warned that those who commit such sins place themselves under the wrath of God. They may or may not taste evil consequences during life; however, after death they surely must answer to God.

3. Growth in love (vv. 9–10)

9 But as touching brotherly love ye need not that I write unto you: for ye yourselves are taught of God to love one another.

10 And indeed ye do it toward all the brethren which are in all Macedonia: but we beseech you, brethren, that ye increase more and more;

God Himself by His Spirit had impressed on the Thessalonians the importance of loving one another. Paul commended them for their faithfulness in doing this. Their love was known throughout the province of Macedonia (mass uh DOH nih uh). Paul had visited two other Macedonian cities, Philippi (FILL ih pigh) and Berea (buh REE uh; Acts 16:11—17:15). People traveled back and forth. Thus their reputation spread. Later when Paul wrote 2 Corinthians 8:1–5, he commended the churches of Macedonia for their sacrificial giving to help believers in faraway Judea.

Paul urged them to continue to grow as they expressed such love. A loving Christian fellowship ought not to be taken for granted. Dangers and temptations constantly threaten believers' love for one another.

4. Necessity for work (vv. 11–12)

11 And that ye study to be quiet, and to do your own business, and to work with your own hands, as we commanded you;

12 That ye may walk honestly toward them that are without, and that ye may have lack of nothing.

When Paul was with the Thessalonians, he taught them to mind their own business and work with their hands. He reemphasized this in verse 11. In 2 Thessalonians 3:6–13, the apostle gave even more emphasis to hard work and minding one's own business. He warned against being lazy busybodies. This seems to have been a special problem among Thessalonian believers.

Because both letters to Thessalonica deal with Paul's teachings about the Lord's coming (1 Thess. 4:13–5:11; 2 Thess. 2), some Bible students think some people there had quit their work because they expected the Lord to come right away. The Bible emphasizes that the way to be ready for the Lord's coming is to be faithfully at work for the Lord, not standing idly looking into heaven (Matt. 24:42–25:46; Acts 1:7–11).

By minding their own business and doing hard, honest work, Christians provide a good testimony before an unbelieving world as well as support themselves.

APPLYING THE BIBLE

1. Hudson Taylor's motto. Hudson Taylor (1832–1905), a pioneer missionary to China, once told a congregation that his life's motto was "Have faith in God" (Mark 11:22). Taylor said that to him the verse meant, "Reckon on God's faith to you."

Hudson Taylor's life was lived daily depending on God's faithfulness. One time, while he was ministering in China, Taylor was asked to come and pray for a man's wife who was near death. Upon arriving at the man's home, Taylor found a room full of sick, starving children. Telling the family how much God loved them, Taylor took out his last coin and gave it to the man. Later in the day, Hudson received a package with money in it for more than he had given the man.

Paul has received good news about the family of the believers at Thessalonica. In verses 6–10 he commended them for it and encouraged them to stand firm in their faith. "Have faith in God' is a good motto for us to follow today.

2. The wonder of love. After Andrew Jackson had retired from military and political life, visitors who entered his room at the Hermitage would find "Old Hickory" sitting before the fire with a Bible in one hand and a picture of his beloved Rachel in the other hand. Her epitaph, which Jackson himself wrote, is carved on her headstone at the Hermitage near Nashville, Tennessee: "Age 61 years. Her face was fair, her person pleasing, her temper amiable, her heart kind. A being so gentle and so virtuous, slander might wound her but could not dishonor. Even death, when he bore her from the arms of her husband, could but transport her to the bosom of her God."

All who read about Jackson know how much he loved his dear Rachel. Paul encouraged the Thessalonian saints to have a deep, abiding love toward each other and all others (vv. 11–13).

3. Sexual immorality. A student on the campus of a leading university responded to a reporter's question about premarital sex in this way: "Why hide it? I have sex with boys. The only difference between me and a lot of other girls on this campus is that I admit it." She is from a small, rural town. She makes good grades and attends church regularly. She dates regularly but says she has had sex with "only seven or eight boys" in her two years at the university.

This is not an isolated case. But God has something to say about sexual immorality, and Paul addresses this sin very strongly in verses 3–8. Each believer must practice the Holy Spirit's command in verse 7: "For God has not called us unto uncleanness, but unto holiness."

4. The worth of work. The great achievers of history have been diligent workers.

▶ Michelangelo frequently slept in his clothes in order to get back to his work without delay. Often he took a block of marble to his bedroom so that he could work on it when sleep eluded him.

▶ John James Audubon apologized for some trifling bit of carelessness in his famous drawing of mockingbirds being attacked by a snake. He explained the sketch was made in Louisiana where the heat was so intense he had to stop after only sixteen hours!

▶ Sir Walter Scott, goaded on by the determination to pay his debts and clear his good name, wrote the "Waverly" novels at the rate of one a month.

▶ President Ulysses S. Grant wrote his memoirs, though he was dying from cancer, in order to leave his family enough money to carry on with their lives.

Almost without exception, men and women in every walk of life have earned success by diligent, hard work. Paul addresses the worth of work in verses 11–12. Laziness is out of character for a Christian.

TEACHING THE BIBLE

▶ *Main Idea:* Christians should live in love and holiness.

▶ *Suggested Teaching Aim:* To lead adults to correct aspects of their lives so they may live in love and holiness.

A TEACHING OUTLINE

1. Use articles you have clipped from newspapers and magazines to create interest.

2. Use a poster you have made to explain "set apart."

3. Use a lesson poster to guide the Bible study.

4. Issue a challenge to members to live holy and pure lives.

Introduce the Bible Study

Cut articles from newspapers and magazines that relate to sexual sins (for example: rape, child abuse, abortion) and place them on a chalkboard or a large sheet of paper. Mount these on a focal wall. **IN ADVANCE,** copy the "Main Idea" on a strip of paper. After mentioning some of the articles, place the strip of paper across the articles and point out that God demands that believers live in love and holiness.

Search for Biblical Truth

On a large map locate Thessalonica. Locate Corinth and indicate that this is where Paul was when he wrote the Thessalonians. Ask members to open their Bibles to 3:11–13 and answer the following questions: What was Paul's attitude toward the Thessalonians? (Loved them— v. 12.) What did Paul want God to do for them? (Make them blameless and holy—v. 13.)

Point out the following you have prepared **IN ADVANCE** and ask members to look for these words as they study. Point out that these words apply to all believers.

Set Apart		
Holy	=	those who have been set apart
Saints	=	holy ones
Sanctified	=	process that results from being set apart
Holiness	=	state resulting from being set apart

On a chalkboard or a large sheet of paper make a poster by writing *How to live.* Under it write, *1. Growth in Christian living.* Ask members to read silently 4:1–2. Ask: What instructions do you think Paul had given the Thessalonians when he first preached to them? (Probably the life and teachings of Jesus.) How well were the Thessalonians living up to these teachings? (Well, but Paul encouraged them to continue onward and upward.)

Write, *2. Set apart from sexual sins* on the poster. Ask: What is God's will for believers in the sexual area? Why was this so important in the first century? Is it any less important today?

Use "Studying the Bible" to explain the possible meanings of "vessel" (4:4). Ask members to read this verse in different translations of the Bible.

DISCUSS: How do you react to this statement: Those who have sex outside of marriage are only hurting themselves.

Write, *3. Growth in love* on the poster. Ask: How well were the Thessalonians doing in this area? (Well; the whole province knew of their love for other believers.) How did they show this love? (Likely through gifts for the poor.)

Write, *4. Necessity for work* on the poster. Ask members to read silently 4:11–12. Using "Studying the Bible," explain why Paul likely included this statement on the need to work.

Give the Truth a Personal Focus

Ask: What does it mean to you to live in love and holiness? Briefly review Paul's four statements on the poster. Ask members to suggest other areas they feel should be included in holiness and love. Ask: What aspects of your life do you need to correct so you may live in love and holiness? Do you need to change some aspects of your life drastically? Do you need to continue in the way you are going? Close in prayer for strength for your members to live in holiness and love.

Pray for Others!

Basic Passage: 2 Thessalonians 1:1–12

Focal Passage: 2 Thessalonians 1:1–12

Many of Paul's letters mention prayers for his readers. For example, 1 Thessalonians 3:11–13 describes Paul's prayer for the church at Thessalonica (THESS uh loh NIGH kuh). Near the end of the same letter, he wrote, "Brethren, pray for us" (1 Thess. 5:25). In a similar spirit, Paul began 2 Thessalonians with thanks for his readers and a prayer for them.

▶**Study Aim:** *To describe Paul's prayer of thanksgiving and intercession for the Thessalonians*

STUDYING THE BIBLE

OUTLINE AND SUMMARY
  I. Greeting (2 Thess. 1:1–2)
 II. Thanksgiving and Prayer (2 Thess. 1:3–12)
     1. Thanksgiving for the Thessalonians (vv. 3–4)
     2. The righteous judgment of God (vv. 5–10)
     3. Prayer for the Thessalonians (vv. 11–12)

Paul sent greetings to the church at Thessalonica (vv. 1–2). He was fully justified in thanking God for their growing love and faith in the face of persecution (vv. 3–4). The evidence of God's righteous judgment was twofold: the preparation of God's people for the coming kingdom and the justice meted out to unbelievers when Christ comes (vv. 5–10). Paul prayed that God would fulfill His calling in His people and hasten the time when Christ would be glorified in and with His people (vv. 11–12).

I. Greeting (2 Thess. 1:1–2)

1 Paul, and Silvanus [sihl VAY nuhs], and Timotheus [tih MOH thih uhs], unto the church of the Thessalonians in God our Father and the Lord Jesus Christ:

2 Grace unto you, and peace, from God our Father and the Lord Jesus Christ.

Ancient letters began with the writer's name. This is one of the thirteen New Testament letters that begins with the name "Paul." In his two letters to Thessalonica, Paul included his two fellow missionaries in the greeting. Paul was clearly the writer, but all three shared in greetings, prayers, and concern for the church. Silas ("Silvanus" was another form of the same name) and Timothy (or "Timotheus") had been with Paul on his visit to Thessalonica (Acts 17:14), and Paul sent Timothy back on a special mission (1 Thess. 3:2, 6).

The church's geographic location was in Thessalonica, but its spiritual state was "in God our Father and the Lord Jesus Christ." Paul, who shared the same spiritual state, sent the twofold greeting of grace and peace. This greeting is found in most of Paul's letters. It uses the typical

Jewish greeting of "peace." Instead of the usual Greek greeting "hail" (*charein*), Paul used the word "grace" (*charis*).

Second Thessalonians was written only a few months after 1 Thessalonians. Paul probably had received some information about how the church was faring. His second letter focused on three issues: persecution (2 Thess. 1), the second coming (2 Thess. 2), and work (2 Thess. 3). He had written about these three subjects in his first letter, but Paul felt that the church needed continued help in these areas.

II. Thanksgiving and Prayer (2 Thess. 1:3–12)

1. Thanksgiving for the Thessalonians (vv. 3–4)

3 We are bound to thank God always for you, brethren, as it is meet, because that your faith groweth exceedingly, and the charity of every one of you all toward each other aboundeth;

4 So that we ourselves glory in you in the churches of God for your patience and faith in all your persecutions and tribulations that ye endure:

Most of Paul's letters begin with a word of gratitude for his readers. Paul thanked God for their growth in faith and in love for one another. In his first letter, Paul had expressed the desire to help perfect what was lacking in their faith (3:10); and he prayed that their love for one another might grow (3:12). Verse 3 of the second letter shows that Paul's desire and prayer had been answered. Their faith had grown exceedingly, and their love for one another abounded.

The words "bound" and "meet" indicate that Paul felt that such thanks for them were fully justified. Paul had commended them for their faith, love, and hope in 1 Thessalonians 1:3. Perhaps some of them had said that Paul had overstated their virtues. Second Thessalonians 1:3 may have been Paul's way of replying that such thanks were not only justified but also needed. (Although he did not mention the word "hope," he wrote of their steadfastness in v. 4.)

Paul said that he praised the Thessalonians as he went to other churches. He praised them specifically for their perseverance and trust amid persecution and afflictions. During Paul's visit, enemies in the synagogue had run him out of town and even pursued him to a neighboring town (Acts 17:1–13). In his first letter, Paul wrote of persecution of the Thessalonians from fellow countrymen (1 Thess. 2:14). The Thessalonian believers had persevered through such times because of their faith in God.

The word "patience" referred not to passive waiting but active perseverance and endurance of trouble. The word "faith" referred here to the trust in God that sustains believers during times of trouble. Although times of trouble tempt believers to doubt that God knows and cares, faith keeps us in touch with God's goodness and power.

2. The righteous judgment of God (vv. 5–10)

5 Which is a manifest token of the righteous judgment of God, that ye may be counted worthy of the kingdom of God, for which ye also suffer:

6 Seeing it is a righteous thing with God to recompense tribulation to them that trouble you;

In times of persecution, believers sometimes doubt that God is just. God's people suffer while their persecutors prosper. Paul cited two evidences of the righteous judgment of God: (1) God would use their faith amid suffering to prepare His people for the coming kingdom. (2) God would mete out justice to those who persecute others.

The New Testament teaches that perseverance through troubles can enable believers to grow in faith, love, and hope (see Matt. 5:10–12; Rom. 5:3–5; 1 Pet. 1:6–8; James 1:2–3). This teaching lies back of verses 4–5. The persecuted believers needed to take the long look. At the time, all they could see were the power and brutality of their persecutors. But Christian hope promised that their perseverance was helping prepare them to be counted worthy of the kingdom of God.

To be counted worthy of the kingdom does not imply that they would earn their entrance into God's kingdom. When we believe, God's grace counts us worthy although we are unworthy. But His grace continues to work in us to show how God can prepare His people for His coming kingdom.

God's righteousness will also be shown in how He renders righteous judgment on those who have persecuted His people. In a world filled with injustice, many people echo the sentiment in the popular saying, "There ain't no justice." However, a just God rules this universe. In the end, accounts will be set right. Justice will finally prevail.

7 And to you who are troubled rest with us, when the Lord Jesus shall be revealed from heaven with his mighty angels,

"Rest" is one of the Bible words to describe the future state of the blessed (see Heb. 4:9). Just as God promised to lead Israel into a land of rest, so He promises a place of eternal rest for His people. Revelation 21:4 promises a new heaven and new earth in which there will be no more pain, sorrow, and death. Revelation 14:13 describes those in Christ as resting from their labors.

The future coming of Christ was a key theme in both letters to Thessalonica (1 Thess. 4:13–5:11; 2 Thess. 2). Verse 7 refers to Christ's coming as a revelation. Christians have already responded to God's revelation through faith. At His future coming, Christ will be revealed so that all can see Him.

8 In flaming fire taking vengeance on them that know not God, and that obey not the gospel of our Lord Jesus Christ:

9 Who shall be punished with everlasting destruction from the presence of the Lord, and from the glory of his power;

When Christ is revealed at His coming, He will be revealed in judgment on those who have rejected the good news. The word "vengeance" has none of the vindictiveness associated with human revenge. It is a compound word based on the same root as the word "righteous" in verses 5 and 6. God's judgment will be the application of unwavering justice by the Judge of the universe.

Those judged will be those who know not God and disobey the gospel of Christ. Both descriptions refer to people who have had opportunities to know God or to respond to the gospel, but they have chosen not to know God or to obey the message of Christ. God's wrath abides on those who could have known God but deliberately rejected Him (Rom. 1:18–32).

Their fate will be eternal separation from God's presence and glory. They will reap what they have sown. They rejected God. They thus chose a destiny deprived of the presence of God.

> **10 When he shall come to be glorified in his saints, and to be admired in all them that believe (because our testimony among you was believed) in that day.**

Verse 10, like verses 5–6a, focuses on the positive aspects of the Lord's coming. Christ will be glorified not only by His saints but in His saints. That is, the saving and transforming work of Christ shall be evident in the lives of the redeemed people of God. The redeemed will join the heavenly chorus in glorifying the Redeemer (see Rev. 5). Paul reminded the Thessalonians that this salvation began for them when they believed the testimonies of the missionaries.

3. Prayer for the Thessalonians (vv. 11–12)

> **11 Wherefore also we pray always for you, that our God would count you worthy of this calling, and fulfil all the good pleasure of his goodness, and the work of faith with power:**

> **12 That the name of our Lord Jesus Christ may be glorified in you, and ye in him, according to the grace of our God and the Lord Jesus Christ.**

Paul prayed that what he had just described would come to pass. He was looking toward the coming of Christ and was praying that the Thessalonians might arrive at the point unto which God was leading them. As noted in comments on verse 5, being counted worthy of the kingdom does not imply that they were to earn entrance into the kingdom. It referred to the completion of God's work of grace in them, which would be revealed at the Lord's future coming.

God places within believers a desire for goodness and for faithful service. Paul prayed that God would fulfill these God-given impulses in the Thessalonians.

Verse 12 links with verse 10. Verse 10 predicted the future glorification of Christ in His people. Verse 12 prayed for that day to come. When Christ is glorified, so will His people be glorified in Him. Back of it all is the grace of God and the Lord Jesus Christ. All praise to Him!

APPLYING THE BIBLE

1. Grace is free. Then-colonel Theodore Roosevelt wanted to buy some delicacies for wounded troops in Cuba during the Spanish American War. He approached Clara Barton, founder of the Red Cross. When his offer was refused, he was troubled and asked what he might do to get the food he wanted. "Just ask for it," Roosevelt was told. "Oh," Roosevelt said, breaking into a big smile. "Then I do ask for it."

God's grace is free to each of us. Although it cost Him everything, even His only begotten Son, it is free to us for the taking.

Paul's greeting to the Thessalonian saints is that they might have "grace and peace" (v. 2). God has nothing better to give.

2. Thanksgiving for others. Here is a good spiritual exercise in which to engage: One day recently when I was reading my Bible and praying, I tried to remember the names of people who had made a significant contribution to my Christian life and thank God for them. I began with my parents who, early in my life, put beneath me a strong Christian foundation. I then thanked God for the Sunday School teachers who had first taught me the Scriptures. I then moved on to thank God for college professors, seminary professors, and people I served as pastor who impacted my life for good. I was amazed at how many have contributed to my life in Christ.

In verses 3–4, Paul gave thanks to God for the Thessalonian believers whom he clearly loved. He thanked God for their steadfast, growing faith and their abounding love for each other. Indeed, "It is a good thing to give thanks unto the Lord" (Ps. 92:1).

3. Which? According to one story, the theologian Augustine (A.D. 354–430) was annoyed by his neighbor. "O Lord," he prayed, "take away this wicked person." And God answered, "Which?" (Augustine or the neighbor!)

The Thessalonian Christians were suffering for their faith, and Paul wrote to comfort them (v. 5), assuring them that the day will come when the scales will be balanced. Our lesson writer says, "Paul cited two evidences of the righteous judgment of God: (1) God would use their faith amid suffering to prepare His people for the coming kingdom; and (2) God would mete out justice to those who persecute others."

God knows which will be rewarded and which will be punished. The Judgment Day will reveal the *which*.

4. Talk to the Shepherd. An elderly woman who had seen a great deal of trouble, but never complained, was much beloved in her community. One day as her pastor was visiting in her home, he asked, "Do you have any trouble sleeping?"

"Not much," answered the aged saint. "When I can't sleep I don't count sheep. I talk to the Shepherd!" Good advice.

Paul talks to the Great Shepherd about His sheep in Thessalonica. He prays that they will live in such a manner that Jesus will be glorified (vv. 11–12).

TEACHING THE BIBLE

▶ *Main Idea:* Christians should pray for others who are experiencing tragedy in their lives.

▶ *Suggested Teaching Aim:* To lead adults to commit to pray for someone who is experiencing tragedy.

1. Use thought questions to relate to members' lives.
2. Use a lesson outline poster to guide the Bible study.
3. Use a commitment card to encourage members to pray for someone experiencing tragedy.

Introduce the Bible Study

Read the following statements: "Why did God allow this to happen?" "All suffering is the result of sin." "Why do evil people prosper when good people suffer?" Ask members to share their reactions to these questions. Point out that the lesson seeks to answer some of the questions we have about suffering and to encourage us to pray for those suffering.

Search for Biblical Truth

Ask a volunteer to read aloud 2 Thessalonians 1:1. Ask members to identify (1) who wrote the letter (Paul, Silas and Timothy), (2) to whom it was written (Thessalonian church), and (3) where the church was located (in Thessalonica geographically but in God spiritually). Ask all members to turn to 1 Thessalonians 1:1. Ask a member to read aloud 2 Thessalonians 1:1 as members look at 1 Thessalonians. Ask: What is the difference in the first part of the verse? (No difference.)

On a chalkboard or a large sheet of paper make a lesson outline poster by writing, *Thanksgiving and Prayer.* Under the heading write, *1. Thanksgiving for the Thessalonians.* Ask a volunteer to read 1:3–4. Ask: For what did Paul express gratitude to the Thessalonians? (Growth in faith and love for one another.) Use "Studying the Bible" to explain Paul's use of "patience" and "faith" (v. 4).

On the poster write, *2. The righteous judgment of God.* Ask a volunteer to read verses 5–10. Using "Studying the Bible," present a brief lecture in which you cover the following points: (1) the two evidences Paul cited of God's righteous judgment; (2) the New Testament teaching that perseverance through troubles can enable believers to grow in faith, love, and hope; (3) what "counted worthy" (v. 5) means and does not mean; (4) what God's promise of rest (v. 7) means to believers; (5) the meaning of "vengeance" (v. 9); (6) how Christ will be glorified (v. 10).

On the poster write, *3. Prayer for the Thessalonians.* Ask a volunteer to read aloud verses 11–12. Say: "Wherefore" (v. 11) can be interpreted, "With all this in mind"—referring to verses 5–10. Paul prayed that what he had just described would come to pass.

DISCUSS: What can we do to be counted worthy of God's calling? How does our praying for others help them in time of trouble? What should be the purpose of our praying?

Give the Truth a Personal Focus

Ask: How do you feel when Christians suffer and evil people prosper? Why does God allow this to happen? What can we do to help people to whom it is happening?

Suggest that one action they can take is to support these people in prayer. Distribute a small piece of paper to all members and ask them to write the name of a person they know who is experiencing tragedy. Then ask them to write below the name, "I will pray for daily this week" and to sign their name. Challenge members to take seriously this commitment to prayer. At the end of the week, suggest that they drop the person a note to share their prayer support. Close in prayer for both them and the people for whom they will be praying.

Do What Is Right!

Basic Passage: 2 Thessalonians 3:1–18
Focal Passage: 2 Thessalonians 3:1–16

The final part of most of Paul's letters contains challenge and encouragement about various aspects of Christian living. Second Thessalonians 3 is such a section. The heart of the chapter deals with the sin of idleness and the need for work.

▶**Study Aim:** *To compare what Paul said to do with what he said not to do*

STUDYING THE BIBLE

▶**Outline and Summary**
  I. Words About Prayer (2 Thess. 3:1–5)
      1. A personal request for prayer (vv. 1–2)
      2. Confidence and prayer (vv. 3–5)
  II. Words About Work (2 Thess. 3:6–15)
      1. Follow Paul's example and teaching (vv. 6–10)
      2. Avoid being idle busybodies (vv. 11–12)
      3. Keep doing right (v. 13)
      4. Discipline disobedient brothers (vv. 14–15)
  III. Concluding Words (2 Thess. 3:16–18)

Paul asked the Thessalonians to pray for the swift advance of the word of God (vv. 1–2). He expressed confidence in his readers based on the faithfulness of the Lord, and he prayed that they would grow in God's love and Christ's endurance (vv. 3–5). He reminded them of his example and teaching concerning work (vv. 6–10). He commanded idle busybodies to settle down and earn their own living (vv. 11–12). Paul encouraged all not to be weary in doing good (v. 13). He told the church to discipline any member who disobeyed Paul's letter (vv. 14–15). Paul closed with a benediction of peace and grace (vv. 16–18).

I. Words About Prayer (2 Thess. 3:1–5)

1. A personal request for prayer (vv. 1–2)

1 Finally, brethren, pray for us, that the word of the Lord may have free course, and be glorified, even as it is with you:

2 And that we may be delivered from unreasonable and wicked men: for all men have not faith.

Paul made two specific requests for prayer. His primary concern was for the advance of the good news; therefore, he asked them to pray that the word of the Lord might spread rapidly and be glorified. The word translated "have free course" means "run." Paul sometimes used it in comparing the Christian life to a race (1 Cor. 9:24, 26). Psalm 147:15 says, "His word runneth very swiftly." Paul asked them to pray that God's word would swiftly advance like a runner in a race. Paul was not thinking of one spurt of growth but of continued rapid advance for God's word.

The apostle also asked that they pray for his deliverance from perverse and wicked men. On the surface, verse 2 may appear to be a selfish request; however, Paul was concerned for his deliverance in order that he might do his part in the continued advance of the word of God.

2. Confidence and prayer (vv. 3–5)

3 But the Lord is faithful, who shall stablish you, and keep you from evil.

4 And we have confidence in the Lord touching you, that ye both do and will do the things which we command you.

5 And the Lord direct your hearts into the love of God, and into the patient waiting for Christ.

In verses 3–5, Paul expressed his confidence in the Lord and in the Thessalonians; then he prayed for the believers.

In the original language, the final word in verse 2 is "faith" *(pistis),* and the first word in verse 3 is "faithful" *(pistos).* Paul contrasted unbelievers' lack of faith with the faithfulness of the Lord. Because the Lord is faithful, Paul trusted Him to provide a solid foundation for the faith and life of the Thessalonians. Paul was also confident that the Lord would keep them from evil and the evil one. Paul may have been thinking of Matthew 6:10, which uses the same words. Since both verses use "the" with "evil," Jesus and Paul probably meant not just evil in general but the evil one who is the source of evil.

Paul's confidence in the Lord gave him confidence about God's people. Thus Paul expressed confidence that the Thessalonians were doing and would continue to do what Paul had commanded. Paul probably had in mind the subject he dealt with in verses 6–15, but it also included other things. Thus before Paul rebuked some of them for their sins, he expressed confidence that with the Lord's help, they would obey what they had been taught.

Paul prayed that the Lord would provide an open path for their hearts into the love of God and the perseverance of Christ. They would be strengthened by a growing assurance of God's love for them. They would be challenged by the example of the One who steadfastly endured so much for others (compare Heb. 12:1–4).

II. Words About Work (2 Thess. 3:6–15)

1. Follow Paul's example and teaching (vv. 6–10)

6 Now we command you, brethren, in the name of our Lord Jesus Christ, that ye withdraw yourselves from every brother that walketh disorderly, and not after the tradition which he received of us.

Verse 6 introduces the central issue in 2 Thessalonians 3. Apparently the problem he addressed in his first letter had become more serious (1 Thess. 4:11–12). The key word "disorderly" occurs several times in one form or another throughout Paul's discussion (vv. 7, 11; see also 1 Thess. 5:14). Originally the word meant soldiers who broke ranks and thus created disorder. In Paul's day, the word was used of an apprentice who avoided doing assigned work. Later verses confirm that deliberate idleness was the problem Paul had in mind.

He commanded other Christians to avoid close fellowship with a brother guilty of this sin. The word "withdraw" meant to "shorten sail," thus to sail around or give a wide berth to such people. Paul elaborated on this in verses 14–15.

> **7 For yourselves know how ye ought to follow us: for we behaved not ourselves disorderly among you;**
>
> **8 Neither did we eat any man's bread for nought; but wrought with labour and travail night and day, that we might not be chargeable to any of you:**
>
> **9 Not because we have not power, but to make ourselves an ensample unto you to follow us.**

Paul reminded his readers how he, Silas, and Timothy had behaved when they were in Thessalonica. Although they had the right to expect financial support from the church, they had not accepted such support (compare 1 Cor. 9:1–18). Instead they had worked night and day to earn their own living and to preach the gospel. In 1 Thessalonians 2:9, Paul used similar words in refuting the perception that the missionaries were preaching for money. Paul's point in 2 Thessalonians 3:7–9 is that the hard work of the missionaries set an example for the church to follow.

> **10 For even when we were with you, this we commanded you, that if any would not work, neither should he eat.**

When Paul was in Thessalonica, he not only set an example by earning his own living; but he also taught the dignity and necessity of work. The Greeks had a low opinion of work, especially manual labor. Paul shared the biblical view of work as a gift and trust from God.

Part of God's original plan for Adam was to tend the garden of Eden (Gen. 2:15). Part of sin's curse is that it changed fulfilling work into grinding toil (Gen. 3:17–19). The Bible's emphasis on honest work shows that people of faith are expected to seek to fulfill God's original purpose. The Book of Proverbs condemns laziness and commends work (Prov. 6:6–11; 18:9). Jesus said, "My Father worketh hitherto, and I work" (John 5:17). Paul's words in 2 Thessalonians 3:10 contain one of the key Bible commands about work.

One word of caution is in order. Paul did not intend to overlook legitimate needs for help from those who were able to work. In fact, Ephesians 4:28 is probably Paul's most complete statement about work: "Let him that stole steal no more: but rather let him labour, working with his hands the thing that is good, that he may have to give to him that needeth." Christians are not to engage in any form of dishonesty or theft. Instead they are to work with their hands to produce what is good. This work is not only to provide support for themselves but also to provide money with which to help the needy.

Paul was writing about those who deliberately avoided opportunities for work. Such people shouldn't expect to be cared for by the hard-working members of the fellowship.

3. Avoid being idle busybodies (vv. 11–12)

11 For we hear that there are some which walk among you disorderly, working not at all, but are busybodies.

Paul had heard that some believers had quit their jobs and were thus causing a problem in the fellowship. These idlers were probably the same group mentioned in 2 Thessalonians 2:1–2. Some church members were unsettled and alarmed at the teaching that the coming of Christ was at hand. The problem of 2 Thessalonians 3:11 probably grew out of such confusion about the second coming. Paul taught that the Lord was coming and that Christians should live in light of that hope (1 Thess. 4:13–5:11; Phil. 3:21; 4:5). He followed Jesus in teaching that we don't know when the Lord is coming and that the way to be ready is to continue to be faithful in service (Matt. 24:36–25:46).

Throughout history, some groups have quit their jobs in expectation of the Lord's immediate coming. This was probably what was going on in Thessalonica. We cannot know for sure their excuses for not working; we do know that they were not working and that they had become busybodies. In Greek, the two words are from the same root. Thus Paul said that they were "not busy, but busybodies." Not only were they a financial burden for the church but they also created confusion and discord. They may have been spreading false ideas about the second coming, or they may have simply become people whose idleness led to gossiping and butting into the lives of others.

12 Now them that are such we command and exhort by our Lord Jesus Christ, that with quietness they work, and eat their own bread.

Paul expected his letter to be read to the congregation. Thus he wrote directly to the idle busybodies. He commanded and exhorted them in the Lord's name. They were to settle down and do their own work. In this way, they were to earn their own living. This seems to be the meaning of the words "eat their own bread."

3. Keep doing good (v. 13)

13 But ye, brethren, be not weary in well-doing.

Verse 13 was addressed to the members of the church who were already working hard. Paul knew that they might be tempted to grow frustrated and slack off in their own faithfulness. This is a constant temptation to those in any church who constantly bear the burdens of others. Paul wrote a similar encouragement in Galatians 5:9. His words follow the command about fulfilling one's own job and bearing one another's burdens (Gal. 5:2, 5).

4. Discipline disobedient brothers (vv. 14–15)

14 And if any man obey not our word by this epistle, note that man, and have no company with him, that he may be ashamed.

15 Yet count him not as an enemy, but admonish him as a brother.

Paul instructed the church to discipline any member who disobeyed what the apostle commanded. Exactly what he meant is not clear, but

Paul told them not to associate with such a one. Paul was careful to remind them that the member was still a brother in Christ and that the purpose of discipline was to make the disobedient brother ashamed. Such shame hopefully would lead him to repent and obey the Lord's word.

III. Concluding Words (2 Thess. 3:16–18)

16 Now the Lord of peace himself give you peace always by all means. The Lord be with you all.

Paul authenticated the letter by writing the closing words with his own hand (v. 15; Rom. 16:22 shows that Paul ordinarily dictated and someone else penned the words). As Paul began with a greeting of grace and peace (2 Thess. 1:2), he closed with a benediction of grace and peace (vv. 16,18). The source of all true grace and peace is the Lord Himself. Thus Paul prayed that the Lord would be with them.

APPLYING THE BIBLE

1. "On your knees, man!" George Adam Smith (1856–1942), English minister and theologian, tells of climbing the 14,804 foot Weisshorn mountain of Switzerland. When he was near the summit, he started in his enthusiasm to stand up to view the majestic scenery below. His guide seized him, pulled him down, and shouted above the roar of the wind, "On your knees, man! In a place like this, you must stay on your knees!"

What a word for the church today. The church must be a praying church in order to have victory in its work for the kingdom of God.

In verses 1–5, Paul pleads for the prayers of the church to strengthen him and expresses his confidence that their prayers will assure victory in their ministry for Jesus.

2. Our best work. Bertel Thorvaldsen (1770–1844) was Denmark's greatest sculptor. On one occasion he was asked, "Which is your greatest statue?" Promptly he replied, "My next one!"

Any work we do with our hands or our minds, from cleaning house to running a great corporation, ought to be work done for God's glory. Remembering that our hands and minds are the hands and mind of Christ ministering to our hurting world, our work ought to be done to the best of our ability. In verses 6–10, Paul encourages the Thessalonian saints to stay busy with their work for God's glory.

3. Busybodies. American writer Washington Irving, some of whose stories contained such personalities as Rip Van Winkle and Ichabod Crane, said that a sharp tongue is the only tool whose edge grows small with constant use. English pastor Charles H. Spurgeon lamented that some people's tongues are sharper than their teeth. Each of us knows that many a blunt word has a sharp edge!

When Colonel Risner was a prisoner during the Vietnam War, he gargled with lye water, hoping that it would so sear his vocal chords that he would be unable to broadcast propaganda when forced to by the enemy.

Paul warns the Thessalonians not to be busybodies. Apparently some members of that church were not content with being miserable; they wanted to make everybody else miserable by spreading gossip that hurt their fellow believers. Paul tells them to stop it (v. 11).

If we will occupy ourselves with the tasks God has assigned to us, we won't have time to "nose in" on the business of others.

4. The worth of work. Paul has a good bit to say in his epistles about the worth of work. There is a godlike quality about honest work. As God worked in creation, so we are to dedicate ourselves to honorable work.

One such person who magnified the worth of work was John Milton (1608–1674). This English author distinguished himself at Cambridge as a scholar. He had a full life serving others in public service. But consider him in his later years. He had grown old. Pain and ill health were his constant companions. Imagine his hands, knotted and gnarled by arthritis. He suffered the torture of gout. In addition, he was blind. What was he to do? Give up? No, in his blindness and beset by other afflictions, he produced *Paradise Lost* and *Paradise Regained* as well as other noted works of literature.

Paul tells the saints at Thessalonica to give themselves to their work. He commands the idle busybodies in the church to work with quietness "and eat their own bread."

TEACHING THE BIBLE

▶ *Main Idea:* True believers will pray and work so that neither aspect is neglected.

▶ *Suggested Teaching Aim:* To lead members to identify aspects of their prayer and work life that need to be improved.

A TEACHING OUTLINE

1. Use a thought question to introduce the Bible study.

2. Use a lesson outline poster to guide the Bible study.

3. Use questions-answers and group discussion to explain the Scripture.

4. Use thought question and listing to give the truth a personal focus.

Introduce the Bible Study

On a chalkboard or a large sheet of paper, **IN ADVANCE** write: "Who do you know who is so heavenly minded that he or she is of no earthly use?" Without letting them name names, ask: How do you feel about persons like this? Are they beneficial to the kingdom of God? Say, Paul addressed a similar problem in Thessalonica.

Search for Biblical Truth

Ask members to open their Bibles to 2 Thessalonians 3:1. **IN ADVANCE,** prepare the following strip posters or write the statements on a chalkboard or a large sheet of paper:

I. Words About Prayer (2 Thess. 3:1–5)

II. Words About Work (2 Thess. 3:6–15)

Place the title and the first point on the focal wall before the class. Ask a volunteer to read 2 Thessalonians 3:1–5. Use the following questions to guide the study. Ask: What were Paul's two specific requests for prayer in 3:1–2? (That the word of the Lord might spread swiftly; that Paul might be delivered from wicked people.) How did Paul contrast wicked men in verse 2b and the Lord in verse 3a? (Wicked do not have faith; the Lord is faithful.) What was Paul's attitude toward the Thessalonians' response to his instructions? (Believed they would fulfill them.)

Place the second poster strip on the wall beneath the first outline point. Ask a volunteer to read 3:6–15. Use "Studying the Bible" to explain "walketh disorderly" and how Paul suggested that the Thessalonians respond to those who would not work. Suggest that apparently some of the people were so wrapped up in anticipating Christ's second coming that they had quit their jobs and were having to be supported by the rest of the church. Ask members to search these verses and find Paul's statement concerning how they were to treat these people. (Verse 10b.)

Say: Apparently the Thessalonians had moved from not working to sitting around gossiping. Use "Studying the Bible" to show the relation between "busy" and "busybodies."

DISCUSS: What right do people who want to be religious have to expect others to support them? Does this mean that churches should not support church staffs?

Ask: What did Paul say we are to do to those who are acting "disorderly"? (Discipline them.) How are we to treat such people? (As friends.)

DISCUSS: Is church discipline outdated? Should churches practice it today? Under what circumstances?

Give the Truth a Personal Focus

Ask: What should be the balance between spending time in religious activities and working to earn a living? How can we tell when one area is interfering with the other? Which is worse, to be so heavenly minded that we are of no earthly use or to be so earthly minded that we are of no heavenly use?

Distribute paper and pencils to members and ask them to list areas of their work or prayer life that need to be improved. Point out that an imbalance in either area is not in keeping with God's plan for His people. Encourage members to bring the two areas into balance.

The Resurrection Hope

Basic Passages: Matthew 28:1–10; 1 Thessalonians 4:13–18
Focal Passages: Matthew 28:1–10; 1 Thessalonians 4:13–18

The Christian hope of victory over death is based on the death and resurrection of Christ. This study combines two passages: one focuses on the resurrection of the Lord, and the other points to the future resurrection of believers.

▶**Study Aim:** *To testify to the Christian hope of victory over death based on the resurrection of Christ*

STUDYING THE BIBLE

OUTLINE AND SUMMARY

I. The Resurrection of Christ (Matt. 28:1–10)
　1. The empty tomb (vv. 1–4)
　2. The angel's message (vv. 5–7)
　3. The risen Lord (vv. 8–10)

II. The Resurrection of Believers (1 Thess. 4:13–18)
　1. The basis for Christian hope (vv. 13–14)
　2. Hope for living and dead believers (vv. 15–17)
　3. Comfort one another (v. 18)

An angel rolled away the stone from the tomb (Matt. 28:1–4). The angel told the women that Jesus had been raised from the dead (Matt. 28:5–7). Jesus Himself appeared to the women (Matt. 28:8–10). The death and resurrection of Jesus provide the basis for confident hope of victory over death (1 Thess. 4:13–14). When Christ comes, the dead in Christ will rise and be gathered up together with living believers to meet the Lord (1 Thess. 4:15–17). Christians should comfort one another with these words (1 Thess. 4:18).

I. The Resurrection of Christ (Matt. 28:1–10)

1. The empty tomb (vv. 1–4)

1 In the end of the sabbath, as it began to dawn toward the first day of the week, came Mary Magdalene [MAG duh lene] and the other Mary to see the sepulchre.

2 And, behold, there was a great earthquake: for the angel of the Lord descended from heaven, and came and rolled back the stone from the door, and sat upon it.

3 His countenance was like lightning, and his raiment white as snow:

4 And for fear of him the keepers did shake, and became as dead men.

Mary Magdalene and another Mary came to the tomb of Jesus about dawn on the first day of the week. Mark 16:1 identifies the other Mary as "the mother of James" and says they came to anoint the body of Jesus.

After Jesus was buried, these two women had been there when a great stone was rolled across the door (Matt. 27:60–61).

Verse 2 describes a great earthquake and the angel of the Lord coming from heaven, rolling away the stone, and sitting on it. These were signs that God had raised Jesus from the dead.

The enemies of Jesus had stationed guards at the tomb to keep anyone from stealing the body (Matt. 27:62–66). When the events of Sunday morning took place, the guards were terrified and fell to the ground as if they were dead.

2. The angel's message (vv. 5–7)

5 And the angel answered and said unto the women, Fear not ye: for I know that ye seek Jesus, which was crucified.

6 He is not here: for he is risen, as he said. Come, see the place where the Lord lay.

7 And go quickly, and tell his disciples that he is risen from the dead; and, behold, he goeth before you into Galilee [GAL ih lee]; there shall ye see him: lo, I have told you.

The angel spoke to the women, telling them not to be afraid. Then he made the joyful announcement that Jesus was no longer in the tomb because He had been raised from the dead. The angel reminded them that Jesus had predicted His resurrection. As confirmation of his message, the angel told the women to look into the tomb. As someone has observed, the stone was not rolled away to let Jesus out but to let in those who came to the tomb.

Then the angel told them to go quickly to the disciples and tell them that Jesus had been raised from the dead. The women also were to tell the disciples that the Lord Himself was going before them into Galilee, where they would see Him for themselves. The disciples were to be reminded that all of this was just as Jesus had earlier predicted (see Matt. 26:32).

3. The risen Lord (vv. 8–10)

8 And they departed quickly from the sepulchre with fear and great joy; and did run to bring his disciples word.

9 And as they went to tell his disciples, behold, Jesus met them, saying, All hail. And they came and held him by the feet, and worshipped him.

10 Then said Jesus unto them, Be not afraid: go tell my brethren that they go into Galilee, and there shall they see me.

The women obeyed the angel and ran quickly to spread the word. Because of what they had seen and heard, the women felt a mixture of fear and joy. As they ran, they met Jesus Himself. When He greeted them, they grabbed His feet and worshiped Him. Because they were still afraid, Jesus tried to calm their fears. He told them to deliver the same message that the angel earlier had given them.

The disciples were to go to Galilee, where they would see Jesus. Matthew's account does not rule out the appearances in Judea (joo DEE uh) recorded in Luke 24 and John 20, but does prepare the way for Jesus' later appearances back in Galilee, where most of His ministry had taken place (John 21; Matt. 28:16–20).

II. The Resurrection of Believers (1 Thess. 4:13–18)

1. The basis for Christian hope (vv. 13–14)

13 But I would not have you to be ignorant, brethren, concerning them which are asleep, that ye sorrow not, even as others which have no hope.

14 For if we believe that Jesus died and rose again, even so them also which sleep in Jesus will God bring with him.

Paul seems to have placed special emphasis on the future coming of Christ when he first preached to the Thessalonians. The doctrine is mentioned throughout his letters to them. After his visit, a question arose in the minds of the believers. Paul received word, probably from Timothy (3:1–6), that they had questions about the dead in Christ. Apparently they had expected Christ to come while all of them were still alive. After some died before His coming, the survivors wondered if the dead would share fully in the Lord's coming and glory.

The dead are referred to as "asleep" (see also v. 15). This was a normal way of speaking of the dead in ancient society. In fact, our word *cemetery* comes from the word translated "asleep." Unbelievers used the word to describe the appearance of the dead, who look as if they are asleep. Most people of the first century had no hope of life after death; therefore, they did not expect anyone to awake from this final sleep.

Christians used the word, but always with the expectation that the dead would awaken (compare Luke 8:49–56; John 11:11–15, 25–26, 43–44). Thus Paul referred to those who "sleep in Jesus" as having victory over death because of the death and resurrection of Jesus Christ.

"Those who have no hope" were the people who did not know Christ. Elsewhere Paul described them as "having no hope, and without God in the world" (Eph. 2:20). This does not mean that they didn't have various human and religious hopes. Some—although only a few—even claimed to believe in some kind of existence beyond death. However, whatever their hopes, they had no real hope because they did not know God and the crucified and risen Lord Jesus Christ.

Thus they grieved in hopeless despair when loved ones died. Christians also grieve when their loved ones die, but our human feelings of grief are comforted by the sure hope of victory over death for us and all who know the Lord. The basis for our confident hope is spelled out in verse 14. The word "if" should be translated "since." Neither Paul nor his readers questioned that Jesus had died and been raised from the dead. Paul assured them that this was the basis for assurance that those who sleep in Jesus will share the coming glory.

2. Hope for living and dead believers (vv. 15–17)

15 For this we say unto you by the word of the Lord, that we which are alive and remain unto the coming of the Lord shall not prevent them which are asleep.

Paul cited the Lord as authority for what he wrote in verse 15. Since this saying is not in the Gospels, it may have been a special revelation of Christ to Paul. Or it could have been a saying of Jesus that was not recorded in the Gospels (for example, see Acts 20:35; John 20:30; 21:25).

The word of the Lord makes this promise: believers who are alive when Christ comes will not precede the dead in Christ. The meaning of the word "prevent" has changed. When the translation known as the King James Version was made, the word meant "precede" or "go before," which is the meaning of the Greek word it translates.

> **16 For the Lord himself shall descend from heaven with a shout, with the voice of the archangel, and with the trump of God: and the dead in Christ shall rise first.**

> **17 Then we which are alive and remain shall be caught up together with them in the clouds, to meet the Lord in the air: and so shall we ever be with the Lord.**

Christ's coming will be accompanied by a shout, a voice of an archangel, and a trumpet blast (compare Matt. 24:31; 1 Cor. 15:52). When Christ comes, the dead in Christ will rise first. Verse 15 assured the Thessalonians that when Christ comes, living believers will not go before the dead in Christ. Verse 16 states the same truth in a different way. Before the living are caught up to glory, something happens first. The dead in Christ are raised. Then after the dead in Christ are resurrected, they will join living believers; and both groups will be caught up together to meet the Lord in the air.

Paul stuck to the main issue with the Thessalonians, and thus he did not answer all our questions about the coming of Christ and the resurrection of believers. Other passages deal with some of the questions. For example, 1 Corinthians 15 contains Paul's description of the resurrection body.

One of the first questions asked by modern readers about 1 Thessalonians 4:13–18 is, "What about the state of the dead in Christ before the final resurrection?" Paul believed that the dead in Christ go immediately to be with the Lord. This is implied in the last part of verse 14. God will bring with Him the dead in Jesus. This suggests that the dead in Christ are in some way already with Him, not unconsciously sleeping in the grave. First Thessalonians 5:10 is clearer: Christ "who died for us, that, whether we wake or sleep, we should live together with him." Clearest still is Paul's testimony in Philippians 1:23, where he wrote of his desire "to depart, and to be with Christ."

When such passages are placed alongside passages about the future resurrection, we are reminded that even the dead in Christ look forward to the coming of Christ and the resurrection. They are already with the Lord, but all God's people are not yet there and all God's purposes are not yet fulfilled. Paul did not get into all the questions and details in 1 Thessalonians 4:13–18. He summed up the final outcome of Christ's victory over death with these joyful words: "So shall we ever be with the Lord."

3. Comfort one another (v. 18)

18 Wherefore comfort one another with these words.

Paul wrote to comfort and encourage those who were worried and confused about the dead in Christ. Paul had assured them of victory over death for all believers: dead and living. He had assured them of reunion of living and dead believers when God's purpose is fulfilled. He told them to comfort one another with these words of assurance and hope. Believers in countless generations have found comfort for themselves and others in these inspired words.

APPLYING THE BIBLE

1. The ministry of angels. I suppose more has been said and written about angels in the last decade than ever before. Books about angels have flooded the market. It is interesting to observe that the Bible has more to say about angels than it says about the devil and demons.

In his book *Angels, Angels, Angels,* Billy Graham says that "angels minister to us personally" (Heb. 1:13–14). The New Testament shows how angels personally ministered to Jesus. They announced His birth (Matt. 1:20, 24); named Him (Luke 2:21); protected Him from Herod (Matt. 2:13); and ministered to Him in His temptations (Matt. 1:13). Jesus taught about angels (Matt. 18:10). Angels were available to rescue Him from the cross (Matt. 26:53); opened and guarded His tomb (Matt. 28:2); witnessed His ascension (Acts 1:10–11); and shall return with Him (Matt. 25:31).

Our lessons today focuses on the angel of the Lord who rolled back the stone to open His tomb. This was not done so Jesus could come out but so the unbelieving world could come in!

2. The resurrection of Jesus. The resurrection of Jesus is a well-attested fact of history. Angels saw Him (Matt. 28:5–6); Mary Magdalene and "the other Mary" saw Him (Matt. 28:9–10); the apostles saw Him (1 Cor. 15:6); Paul saw him (1 Cor. 15:8); the Emmaus disciples saw Him (Luke 24:13–32); the seven saw Him (John 21:1–23).

Beyond question, the early Christians believed that Jesus had been raised from the dead. But in spite of the evidence, various theories have been advanced to deny the resurrection of Jesus' body:

▶ The stolen body theory teaches that the disciples stole His body;

▶ The swoon theory teaches that Jesus did not die but only fainted on the cross;

▶ The telegram theory teaches that the spirit of Jesus communicated with the disciples to let them know that He was alive in heaven;

▶ The legend theory teaches that the resurrection was a myth that originated among early Christians;

▶ The hyperbolic theory teaches that Jesus was never raised but that the disciples used such strong language in describing His continuing life that the early church misunderstood what the disciples were saying.[1]

3. The significance of the resurrection. The resurrection declares Jesus to be the Son of God (Rom. 1:4); provides salvation (Rom. 4:25;

1 Cor. 15:17); proves that death is not the end (John 11:25–26); and promises our own resurrection (1 Cor. 15:20). The resurrection is the crowning of Jesus (Phil. 2:8–9).

4. Our resurrection body. Our resurrection body will not be the same as the one laid in the grave (1 Cor. 15:35–38); will not be flesh and blood (1 Cor. 15:50–58); will not be just spirit but will have flesh and bones (Luke 24:39); will be incorruptible (1 Cor. 15:42); will be glorious (1 Cor. 15:43); will be powerful (1 Cor. 15:43); will be heavenly (1 Cor. 15:47–49); will be like the resurrected body of Jesus (1 Cor. 15:49); will be shining and bright as the body of Jesus (Matt. 17:2—because we shall be like Him); and our resurrection shall be the consummation of our redemption (Rom. 8:23).

5. We will look fine. A newspaper correspondent visited former-president Dwight Eisenhower. He was showing his age. Although Eisenhower looked pale and frail, the reporter told the old general that he was looking well. Eisenhower replied, "Well, you know that a man has three ages. There is youth, then middle age, and then the time when everybody says, 'My, how fine you are looking!'"[2]

Our bodies grow old and weak, but the day is coming for each believer when his or her body will be and look just fine!

TEACHING THE BIBLE

▶ *Main Idea:* The resurrection of Christ and believers should influence the way we live daily.

▶ *Suggested Teaching Aim:* To lead adults to identify ways Christ's resurrection and their resurrection affects the way they live.

A TEACHING OUTLINE

1. Use a thought question to relate the Bible study to members' lives.

2. Guide members in developing two facts sheets to help in their search for biblical truths.

3. Use a question and listing to apply the study.

Introduce the Bible Study

Ask: What difference does Easter make in the life of the average non-believer? What difference does it make in your life? What difference has it made this past year? Allow members to respond. Suggest that one way Easter and Jesus' resurrection affect us is to give us hope.

Search for Biblical Truth

IN ADVANCE, provide two small sheets of paper (an 8 1/2-by-11-inch sheet cut in half) for each member. At the top of one write, *Facts Sheet About Christ's Resurrection.* At the top of the other write, *Facts Sheet About the Resurrection of Believers.* Have a large sheet of paper or a chalkboard divided into two columns. Label each column with one of the above headings.

Ask members to open their Bibles to Matthew 28:1–10. Ask members to help you compose a "Facts Sheet About Christ's Resurrection." Let them search these verses and list facts about Jesus' resurrection. Their list will likely differ from the following, but should include these:

▶ It occurred on Sunday morning.

▶ The first people to know that Jesus had been raised were women.

▶ An angel rolled away the stone.

▶ The purpose of rolling away the stone was not to let Jesus out but to let others see in.

▶ Jesus had predicted His resurrection.

▶ Those who had seen that He was risen were to tell others.

▶ Jesus arranged a meeting with His disciples to assure them of His resurrection.

DISCUSS: What difference does it make to you personally that Jesus has risen from the dead? What difference did it make this past week?

Ask members to open their Bibles to 1 Thessalonians 4:13–18. Ask members to help you compose a "Facts Sheet About the Resurrection of Believers." Let them search these verses and list facts about how Paul said the resurrection of believers would take place. Their list will likely differ from the following, but should include these:

▶ Our resurrection is based on Jesus' resurrection.

▶ Christ's coming will be accompanied by a shout, an archangel's voice, and a trumpet blast.

▶ Believers who have died are already with Christ in some form.

▶ Christ will raise those believers who have died first.

▶ Christ will then bring those raised believers and come for those who are living.

▶ Believers living on earth will meet this group in the air.

▶ All believers will be with the Lord forever.

▶ We should comfort each other with these facts.

DISCUSS: What about the state of the dead in Christ before the final resurrection? How does your resurrection affect the way you live in the world?

Give the Truth a Personal Focus

On the facts sheets you have written on the chalkboard or large sheet of paper, write in large letters: SO WHAT?? Ask members to write one way Christ's resurrection will affect the way they live and one way the facts about the resurrection of believers will affect the way they will live. Close in prayer.

---

1. Ray Summers, *The Life Beyond* (Nashville: Broadman Press, 1959), 34–36.

2. Benjamin P. Browne, *Illustrations for Preaching* (Nashville: Broadman Press, 1977), 95.

Respect for Human Life

Basic Passages: Genesis 1:27; Matthew 5:13–16,2 1–22, 27–28, 43–45a

Focal Passages: Genesis 1:27; Matthew 5:13–16, 21–22, 27–28, 43–45a

This is a special lesson for those who want such a lesson on Sanctity of Human Life Sunday. Many Bible passages support sanctity of human life. This lesson builds on the foundational teaching about the source of life in Genesis 1:27 and then examines passages from the Sermon on the Mount about respect for human life.

▶**Study Aim:** *To oppose abortion and all practices that show a lack of respect and appreciation for human life*

STUDYING THE BIBLE

OUTLINE AND SUMMARY
  I. **Source of Life (Gen. 1:27)**
 II. **Respect for Life (Matt. 5:13–16, 21–22, 27–28, 43–45a)**
   1. Role in society (Matt. 5:13–16)
   2. Value of human life (Matt. 5:21–22)
   3. Purity in relationships (Matt. 5:27–28)
   4. Respect in action (Matt. 5:43–45a)

God created male and female human beings in His own image (Gen. 1:27). Believers are so to live that their lives serve as an example that leads others to lifestyles that are wholesome and beneficial to all (Matt. 5:13–16). Followers of Jesus are neither to take human life nor to indulge emotions that lead to hostile acts (Matt. 5:21–22). Christians are not to commit adultery or even to lust after others (Matt. 5:27–28). Believers are to show their respect for all people by loving them, blessing them, doing good to them, and praying for them (Matt. 5:43–45a).

I. Source of Life (Gen. 1:27)

27 So God created man in his own image, in the image of God created he him; male and female created he them.

The early chapters of Genesis contain foundational teachings for all basic biblical teachings. None is so foundational as that God is the Creator of His good creation, and that human beings were created in God's own image. God breathed the breath of life into all living creatures, but only humans were created in His own image.

Humans are like the rest of creation in many ways, but we are also different in this important respect. We share the image of the God who made us. None of us understands all that this means, but it surely means that we were made with a unique capacity for relating to the God who made us. We are capable of loving and worshiping God.

All life is valuable for the purpose God made it, but human life is supremely valuable because of this capacity for knowing and serving God. After the flood, when God made His covenant with humanity, He based the prohibition of murder on the fact that humans are in the image of God (Gen. 9:6).

II. Respect for Life (Matt. 5:13–16, 21–22, 27–28, 43–45a)

1. Role in society (Matt. 5:13–16)

13 Ye are the salt of the earth: but if the salt have lost his savour, wherewith shall it be salted? it is thenceforth good for nothing, but to be cast out, and to be trodden under foot of men.

14 Ye are the light of the world. A city that is set on an hill cannot be hid.

15 Neither do men light a candle and put it under a bushel, but on a candlestick; and it giveth light unto all that are in the house.

16 Let your light so shine before men, that they may see your good works, and glorify your Father which is in heaven.

Salt was especially valuable in ancient society. It had many uses, but its primary value was as a preservative. As salt was used to preserve food from spoiling and ruin, so were followers of Jesus to be a preserving force in a corrupting society. Disciples of Jesus who fail in this crucial role are judged to be like salt without savor, "good for nothing."

The purpose of light is to shine and enlighten. As Jesus noted, no one lights a candle and then hides its light. Instead, the candle is used so that people might see. A city on a hill cannot be hid if even one candle is shining.

Jesus used these two simple analogies to commission His followers to a crucial role in the world. He called us the "salt of the earth" and the "light of the world." He has given us a crucial task and invested us with a great trust. We are to be a preserving force in the moral decay of a sinful world. We are to shine the light of God's judgment and salvation into the dark corners of life. Examples of moral decay abound: pornography, injustice, exploitation, violence, taking of helpless human life, and a multitude of other evils. Beginning with our own children, other youth, and peers, Christian adults can be salt and light.

Our goal is not to call attention to ourselves, either as reformers or deliverers. Our goal is to be instruments of the God of light in salvation and grace. After all, Jesus said that when they see our good works, they are not to praise us, but to "glorify your Father which is in heaven."

2. Value of human life (Matt. 5:21–22)

21 Ye have heard that it was said by them of old time, Thou shalt not kill; and whosoever shall kill shall be in danger of the judgment:

22 But I say unto you, That whosoever is angry with his brother without a cause shall be in danger of the judgment: but whosoever shall say to his brother, Raca, shall be in

danger of the council: and whosoever shall say, Thou fool, shall be in danger of hell fire.

Jesus cited a number of examples of the demands of the kingdom of heaven that exceeded the traditional morality of the Pharisees (Matt. 5:20). All recognized the prohibition of murder in the Sixth Commandment (Exod. 20:13). Jesus went behind the act of murder to the attitudes that sometimes lead to murder. He condemned harboring wrath in one's heart toward another person. There is such a thing as righteous indignation, but most human anger is selfish and destructive.

Jesus condemned the kind of hatred that results in abusive speech to others. The words translated "raca" and "thou fool" were insulting terms of contempt. Jesus said that those whose hatred was so great courted the judgment of hell just as did those who actually were guilty of murder.

Jesus was not saying that hatred causes the same tragic result as actual murder. He was saying that hatred can lead to murder and that it is sinful even when it doesn't. For example, God warned Cain of murderous thoughts that he needed to control (Gen. 4:6–7). Those thoughts were sinful; but presumably if Cain had heeded God's warning, Abel's life might have been spared. Unfortunately, Cain kept feeding those evil thoughts; and this led him to murder his brother.

Verses 21–22 not only warn against murder and hatred but also affirm that all human beings should be treated with dignity and respect. Human life is taken and people are abused when such respect is missing from people's attitudes and beliefs. Every person—including the pre-born—deserves to be treated with dignity and respect. Such respect begins with every person's right to life, but it also includes the right to a life free from abuse and exploitation.

3. Purity in relationships (Matt. 5:27–28)

27 Ye have heard that it was said by them of old time, Thou shalt not commit adultery:

28 But I say unto you, That whosoever looketh upon a woman to lust after her hath committed adultery with her already in his heart.

Jesus referred to another of the Ten Commandments, the Seventh Commandment (Exod. 20:14). Jesus affirmed the prohibition against adultery. The family is the foundation of society and the basic arena for human relations. Marriage is the foundation for the home. No family can exist without the faithfulness and trust of husband and wife within the one-flesh union of marriage (Gen. 2:24). Thus adultery destroys the fabric of the most sacred of human relations.

As in the case with murder, Jesus went behind the actual act to the attitude and motive. He condemned not only adultery but also looking on another person with lust. Again, Jesus was not saying that lust does the same harm as the actual act of adultery. If that were His point, a man might say, "I am already guilty of lusting after her; I may as well go ahead and commit adultery." Jesus' point was that lust is what feeds sexual immorality; and even when lust doesn't lead to adultery, lust itself is sinful because it reduces another person to a sex object.

Our society pays little attention to what Jesus taught. Several years ago, the press made fun of a presidential candidate who referred to his efforts to honor this particular teaching of Jesus. The prevailing mood of our culture is sexual indulgence and unrestrained sexual activity—before marriage and outside of marriage. As a result, we live in a world where sexually transmitted diseases flourish and where abortions on demand are used as a method of birth control.

At the root of many of these problems is the prevailing view of many people that everyone should be completely free to have sex with any other person. Our culture promotes and popularizes this deadly view by all kinds of attractive propaganda. The sexual promiscuity and outrageous behavior of media figures are proudly displayed for the young to follow. Those who believe the Bible are facing a tremendous challenge in trying to buck this tide, but some progress is being made. Dedicated adults and youth can set an example and present an alternative to the destructive cycle of sexual immorality and all that spawns it.

4. Respect in action (Matt. 5:43–45a)

43 Ye have heard that it hath been said, Thou shalt love thy neighbour, and hate thine enemy.

44 But I say unto you, Love your enemies, bless them that curse you, do good to them that hate you, and pray for them which despitefully use you, and persecute you;

45 That ye may be children of your Father which is in heaven:

Jesus' teachings in the Sermon on the Mount were revolutionary, none more so than His words about loving enemies. Polite society defines love primarily as an emotion and limits the scope of such love to people we like and people who like us. Jesus challenged both the definition and the scope of this view of love. For one thing, Jesus defined love not as something we feel so much as something we do. Christian love, or *agape,* is doing good to others no matter how we may feel about them or how they may feel about us (Luke 6:27–28).

This revolutionary definition of love enables us to enlarge the scope of love to include not only neighbors and friends but also enemies. By definition, our enemies don't like us. They often do things to hurt us. Yet Jesus said that in spite of how they hurt us and make us feel, we still can do good for them. This act of good is Christian love. Jesus pointed out that this is God's kind of love. The Heavenly Father does not love people because they are worthy or because they love Him. Instead He loves us while we are yet sinners (Rom. 5:6–8).

Luke 10:25–37 illustrates Jesus' teaching. The lawyer's question, "Who is my neighbour?" (v. 29) shows that he was trying to limit those to whom he should show love. The Samaritan in Jesus' parable acted in love. He may have felt a mixture of emotions—including fear and revulsion. What counted, however, was what he did. He stopped, helped the injured man, carried him to safety, and paid for his care. He did this for someone he didn't know, but someone who was probably a Jew—an enemy of his people the Samaritans.

Any generation would be revolutionized with Christian love if followers of Jesus practiced Matthew 5:43–45a. As applied to the current turmoil in society about abortion, this passage forces each follower of Christ to face questions about how we should act toward people who hold different views and have taken different actions than we have. How can we act redemptively toward proponents, practitioners, and prospects for abortion?

APPLYING THE BIBLE

1. Someone special. We are special because we were created in God's image (Gen. 1:27). William Gladstone (1809–1898), a devout Christian who served as British Prime Minister, said about man: "Man himself is the crowning wonder of creation; the study of his nature the noblest study the world affords."

Dr. H. H. Hobbs writes: "At the end of the first five stages in creation God saw that it was 'good.' But having made man, he saw that it was 'very good.' This suggests that man is someone special in God's creative act and purpose."[1]

The question, "Where did man come from?" has been raised repeatedly through the ages. The evolutionist answers that man evolved from a lower species of life. But, Hobbs says, "The theory of evolution will never become fact until the so-called 'missing link' between ape and man is found beyond question of doubt. . . . But there is no evidence that a lower species ever climbed to a higher level."[2]

The Christian answer is that God created man in His image—"an exact duplicate," Hobbs states. Therein lies our uniqueness, our "specialness."

2. The destructive power of hate. American lawyer Clarence Darrow (1857–1938) said, "I've never murdered a man, but I have read many an obituary with pleasure."

That's what Jesus is talking about here (vv. 21–22). He is not just condemning the act of murder but also hatred in the heart that produces it. The kingdom of God exceeds traditional morality and demands more. We are to shun even evil thoughts that produce evil deeds!

British novelist Thomas Hardy (1840–1928) wrote: "Sometimes more bitterness is sown in five minutes than can be gotten rid of in a whole lifetime." That's the idea behind Jesus' words. To these thoughts, let me add the remark of the African-American educator Booker T. Washington: "No man can drag me down so low that I will hate him."

The sanctity of human life must not only keep the Christian from taking a life but also from hatred that produces murder.

3. Love of neighbors. A man named Greene was thinking about moving his family to a town named Smithdale. Stopping at a gas station, he asked the elderly attendant, "What kind of people live here? Are they nice and friendly?"

The old gentleman scratched his unshaven chin and asked, "What kind of people live in your town?"

"Oh," said the stranger, "they are the nicest and kindest people you could find anywhere."

"Well," the attendant replied, "you know, that's just the kind of people who live in Smithdale."

Another stranger stopped at the station about a week later and asked the same question. And the attendant asked, "What kind of people live in your town?"

"Oh, they are miserable people, just miserable. They are the most unfriendly, stuck-up folks we ever met. We have been miserable the whole time we have lived there."

"Well," said the old-timer, "I would like to be more encouraging, but that is exactly the kind of people you will find here!"

Our attitude toward others very often determines their attitude toward us (vv. 43–45; Luke 10:25–37).

TEACHING THE BIBLE

▶ *Main Idea:* To show respect for human life.

▶ *Suggested Teaching Aim:* To lead adults to commit themselves to respect for human life.

A TEACHING OUTLINE

1. Use a graffiti wall to introduce the Bible study.

2. Use Scripture search and discussion questions to search for biblical truth.

3. Use a chart to explore the Scripture.

4. Use thought questions to give the truth a personal focus.

Introduce the Bible Study

Place two large sheets of paper on opposite walls. On one write *What is God like?* and on the other write *What are humans like?* As members enter, ask half of them to go to one of the walls and write a brief description to answer the question. Ask the other half to go to the other wall. Begin by reading some of the descriptions. Ask: If we are created in God's image, how should we live? Suggest that today's lesson will help us discover respect for human life.

Search for Biblical Truth

Read aloud Genesis 1:27. Ask: What does the fact that God made "male" and "female" in His image indicate? (Among other things, that the verse does not refer to physical characteristics of God.) How are we like God? How are we like the rest of creation?

DISCUSS: Since humans are made in God's image, what principle or principles can you draw from that fact?

Read aloud Matthew 5:13–16. Ask: What do you think Jesus meant by calling His followers the salt of the earth and the light of the world?

DISCUSS: What can you do in your family to fulfill your role as "salt of the earth" and "light of the world"? What can you do in the world?

Read aloud Matthew 5:21–22. On a chalkboard or a large sheet of paper write, *You have heard . . . but I say to you.* Under the first phrase write *Do not murder.* Point out that this is what the Sixth Commandment said (Exod. 20:13). Ask: What did Jesus say to do? (Don't be angry with anyone.) Write this under the last part of the heading.

DISCUSS: What principle can we draw from these verses about how we should relate to people?

Read aloud Matthew 5:27–28. On the chalkboard or large sheet of paper write, *Do not commit adultery.* Point out that this is the Seventh Commandment (Exod. 20:14). Ask: But what did Jesus say to do? (Don't be lustful.) Write this under the last part of the heading. Ask: Why is adultery wrong?

DISCUSS: What principle can we draw from these verses about how we should relate to people? What do they say about abortion?

Read aloud Matthew 5:43–45a. On the chalkboard or large sheet of paper write, *Love your neighbors; hate your enemies.* Ask: What did Jesus say to do? (Love your enemies.) Write this under the last part of the heading.

DISCUSS: What would it do in even one of your relationships if you obeyed this command? What should we do about people who have violated God's laws and showed disrespect for His people? Are we to love them, too?

Give the Truth a Personal Focus

Ask: What can we do to recover the image of God in our lives? How can you show more respect for human life? What should be our response toward those who hold different views and have taken different actions than we have?

Ask members to think of the person they are most angry with. Challenge them to show respect for that person by doing something to heal the anger. Point out that although we cannot change the world, we can change one relationship.

---

1. H. H. Hobbs, *The Origin of All Things* (Waco, Tex.: Word Books, 1975), 25.
2. Ibid., 27.